A TONGUE IN YOUR HEAD

Overheard in the New Cut :

Mother to Child : *Wodjemean, can't s'y? Got a tongue in yer*
'ead, 'aven't yer?

A TONGUE IN YOUR HEAD

BY

L. A. G. STRONG

WITH A FOREWORD BY

J. COMPTON

Director of Education for Ealing

LONDON

SIR ISAAC PITMAN & SONS, LTD.

First Published 1945.

Reprinted 1946

SIR ISAAC PITMAN & SONS, Ltd.
PITMAN HOUSE, PARKER STREET, KINGSWAY, LONDON, W.C.2
THE PITMAN PRESS, BATH
PITMAN HOUSE, LITTLE COLLINS STREET, MELBOURNE
UNITEERS BUILDING, RIVER VALLEY ROAD, SINGAPORE
27 BECKETTS BUILDINGS, PRESIDENT STREET, JOHANNESBURG

ASSOCIATED COMPANIES
PITMAN PUBLISHING CORPORATION
2 WEST 45TH STREET, NEW YORK
205 WEST MONROE STREET, CHICAGO

SIR ISAAC PITMAN & SONS (CANADA), Ltd.
(INCORPORATING THE COMMERCIAL TEXT BOOK COMPANY)
PITMAN HOUSE, 381-383 CHURCH STREET, TORONTO

MADE IN GREAT BRITAIN AT THE PITMAN PRESS, BATH
D6—(E407)

FOREWORD

A WORD on the origin of this book. About a year ago, the Incorporated Association of Teachers of Speech and Drama, whose Chairman I have the honour to be, asked Mr. L. A. G. Strong if he would write a book which would show clearly to the men and women of Great Britain that there are problems relating to the everyday use of our mother speech which are widespread and serious, and offer some guidance on the ways in which we might set about dealing with them. Mr. Strong knew the programme of active work which the Association was undertaking and was in full sympathy with it. He promised to write the book, and here it is.

That is not to say for a moment that this is a book written to order. No one could read a single chapter of it without recognizing that Mr. Strong is writing something that he had to write, something that his experiences have driven him to think about and to feel about. If the I.A.T.S.D. had not asked him to write this book, he would have been obliged to write it for his own peace of mind.

I hope that he will make you realize that we cannot afford, as a people, to go on seeing the general use of spoken English deteriorate. If not, then nothing I can say will matter in the slightest. And indeed, although this is a preface, it ought perhaps to be stuck at the end of the book because my chief purpose in it is to ask a question: when you have finished reading Mr. Strong, and have been excited by his revelations and persuaded by his arguments, what are you going to do? We have gone on far too long easily assuming that the responsibility for trying to cope with the progressive degeneration in speech, everywhere noticeable, rests with the teachers. The teachers in all kinds of schools and institutions have done a magnificent job in this as in other respects against the heaviest handicaps, and it is time we began to understand that unless we work with them and give them all the assistance, direct and indirect, we can, they will be able to make little progress. The problems of our speech are community problems whether we think in terms of small communities or the big community which is the nation.

What *can* we do ? Well, we can do a number of things. We can stress the necessity by any means at our disposal for co-ordinated action. Let us endeavour to persuade the Ministry of Education and the Local Education Authorities to recognize the nature of the problems and undertake together a programme for speech betterment. We ought to be making ourselves various kinds of a nuisance until there are signs that some large-scale action in terms of a well thought-out scheme is being undertaken officially. Then we have our own immediate responsibilities which we can fulfil by seeing that, in the societies and organizations to which we belong, consideration is given to the substance of Mr. Strong's book and some decision reached on what should be done, not by other people, but by the members of the society or organization themselves.

It is time we began to get angry about the badness of the speech we hear all around us. And having got angry, we must think constructively. That is where Mr. Strong is so immensely helpful. He is writing on issues which are living and important and interesting for every one who merits citizenship. If we go on neglecting our heritage much longer, if we continue to use our ears and our tongues badly, a time will come when recovery may be impossible.

J. Compton.

PREFACE

SUPPOSE that you and I meet, and wish to exchange information and ideas. Suppose further that, like me, you use the English language. Splendid. We open our mouths and talk; and — hey presto! — understanding follows. What could be simpler?

Yet this process, apparently so simple, is in fact exceedingly complicated, and there is a great deal in it that can go wrong. I wrote " hey presto " on purpose. It wasn't just a cliché. " Hey presto " used to be the conjurer's invocation to his magic: and if at our first meeting we have understood each other, something magical has happened.

Consider what we have to do. First of all, we have had to be able to recognize the things we want to talk about, and the relationship between them, which is the subject of what we want to say. In other words, we must be able to think coherently about our environment. Then we must know, and be able to utter, the noises which we have agreed —in that extensive agreement known as the English language—shall represent these things and relationships. In order to utter these noises, we have had to set in motion a process of very great complexity, none the less complex for the fact that habit has made us to a large extent unconscious of it. We had to learn how to do it once, slowly, painfully, by imitation, with many tearful and indignant failures : but that was long ago, and it has now become second nature to us.

Yet how complex it is ! We have to draw air into our lungs and release it in such a way that, co-ordinated with certain muscular movements involving our vocal cords, tongue, teeth, lips, and nasal passage, it gives out a recognizable version of the noises, the combination of vowels and consonants, which we wish to make.

In order to do all this, the various parts of the mechanism, from the brain onwards, must be in good working order. If the muscles of my throat are cramped or paralysed, my vocal cords cannot emit a tone. If my vocal cords are damaged, instead of a resonant tone I shall utter a hoarse whisper. If my tongue and lips are not under control, I shall not be able to articulate clearly : you may hear my vowels but not my consonants. Some of these will vanish if my nasal passages are blocked.

If I am nervous, and stammer or mumble : if I swallow my words, and do not distinguish clearly between one vowel and another : if I am too lazy to sound my consonants properly : if, for some physical or psychological cause, the tone of my voice is inappropriate to what I am trying to convey : if I pronounce my words in such a manner as to distract your attention from what I am saying to irrelevant speculations as to the amount of money my father had to spend on my schooling : if the quality of my voice suggests a personality which is distasteful to you : well, the current of understanding between soul and soul is apt to be short-circuited or, to say the least, impaired.

And when the speaking is public, from platform or stage, or is subjected to the merciless close-up of the microphone, these defects and difficulties are greatly magnified.

In short, there is a very great deal that can go wrong, and often does.

This fact, and circumstances arising from it, are considered in the pages that follow. The pages contain a good

deal of repetition. It is deliberate. " 'Arp, 'arp, 'arp ! "
said a friend of ours, in complaint against her brother-in-
law's nagging. The complaint may be extended to me,
but I risk it willingly.

L.A.G.S.

CONTENTS

A TONGUE IN YOUR HEAD

CHAPTER I

He knows me as the blind man knows the cuckoo,
By the bad voice.

MERCHANT OF VENICE.

THE English language is inferior to none in eloquence and in beauty of sound. It is a magnificent instrument for the expression of personality and the communication of meaning, and it belongs to a people whose natural voices are as good as any in the world. The English tradition in vocal music is centuries old, and our poetic inheritance is unrivalled.

All this is true : and the way the average English person speaks is a living denial of every word of it.

To hear the majority of educated English men and women use their language, any one accustomed to listen would suppose it to be a mean and unresonant dialect, poor in vocabulary, limited in expression, graceless in sound, fit only as a medium for the scanty and utilitarian utterance of a race of savages. He would conclude that they were incapable of emotion, and moronic in range of interest : that they could not open their mouths more than half an inch, that their labial muscles were atrophied, their nasal passages blocked, and that they were afflicted with chronic shortness of breath.

You may consider this an exaggeration. I do not. It is true that experience, training, and the attempt to use my own voice have made me sensitive, and that several years of adjudicating at festivals, schools, and colleges have taught me to listen : but I am thinking of the everyday use of the voice, not the specialized : its ordinary function of telling us what its owner is like and what he wants to say. The speech of most English people pitifully misrepresents the language; and their voices pitifully misrepresent their characters. The English character is not clipped, pinched, indecisive, or adenoidal. The range of our interests and emotions is not adequately expressed in a shallow monotone. We do not lead the timid and inhibited lives our speech suggests.

The trouble is not only that we are illiterate, in the sense that we draw hardly at all on the resources of our language, but that we never learn to speak. Unless we choose a profession which calls for the skilled use of the voice, we are not taught to use it. Speaking is not considered a part of English as taught in school. It is possible to get first class honours in English Language and Literature at Oxford or Cambridge and make a noise like the creaking of an outraged wicker chair. The noble prose of the Authorized Version is shamefully distorted in church and cathedral, the professor in the lecture room mumbles a travesty of the lines that move him, innumerable worthies rise to " say a few words " which do not make sense, and could not be heard beyond the third row even if they did.

" Unaccustomed as I am to public speaking "—but he shouldn't be. Public and private speech differ only in scale. What is wrong is that he has never learned to express his thoughts clearly in private. He should never have been allowed to go out into the world with a voice which doesn't express him, which gives a wrong impression to his fellow man.

That we speak our language badly is a matter of general agreement. You do not have to take it from me. More than that, the education authorities have actually started to do something about it : what, they are—at the time of writing—not quite clear. The idea persists that there is something precious and artificial about learning to speak : and the fact that a lack of any standard has enabled bad teachers of so-called elocution to do widespread harm has intensified the natural English suspicion of taking trouble about anything which is not one's profession, or a game. Our cult of the amateur has much to answer for. Those who direct our educational policy are afraid that if children are taught to speak the results will be unnatural. On the contrary, it is natural speaking that needs to be taught : the unhampered use of the voice as an instrument of the mind, to express personality and ideas. Melba once said that it was more natural to sing well than badly. So it is ; but most of us are a long way from Nature, and our education does little to lessen the gap.

The raw material is all right. There is no doubt about that. I have been going to schools of all kinds, all over the country, for the past fourteen years, and I have judged at speech competitions in these schools, and at festivals, hearing trained and untrained voices. The percentage of naturally good voices is high, and has little to do with social class or difference (except in cases where children have not had enough to eat). The characters behind these voices are lively (one learns presently), independent, sensitive, generous, adventurous : but, again and again, the voices do not express them. Something has got in the way, something which a teacher could remove. Not any teacher, but a teacher who understands the relation of character to voice, and the mechanics of speech. A sprinkling of such teachers is at work. There should be one in every school.

The fact that we speak our language badly is due to several causes, but the central one is the imbecile way in which English has been taught in our schools and even in our universities.

English is not a " subject." It is life itself. It is the instrument by which English-speaking people relate themselves to the universe and all that is in it. Our hopes, our fears, our prayers, our inmost thoughts, our communication with other people (except in the universal fields of art and music), our very means of life—all these are English. Our literature, that storehouse of the spirit from which we can enrich our whole response to life, is English.   The creative energy of our minds is English.   English is our life, inner as well as outer.

How have the schools treated it ?   They have made it a " subject," and, till recently, an unimportant one.   Instead of releasing through it a spontaneous flood of energy, they have used it as a cramping and devitalizing discipline.   It has become, not the approach to literature and life, but a series of barriers guarded by boredom and disgust.   You need to work hard to destroy the pleasure fresh young minds can take in story-telling and in poetry, but these lessons have done it.   Dull minds have taken the master-pieces of our language, forced them upon pupils who in any case were not yet ready, robbed them of life and magic, used them as stuff for annotation and the giving of marks.   By these and other means, they have managed to create a fear and hatred of literature and of ideas so real as to have become part of the Englishman's social code.

Admittedly, things are improving : but we have a terribly long way to go.   If our English teaching has lost some of its joylessness, it is still far from creative.   It still falls far short of the child's capacity and perceptions.   There is still much in the most up-to-date teachers' common room to make the creative writer weep.   Few teachers' idea of writing rises above a pedantic avoidance of mistakes.   Few have an ear for rhythm in verse or prose, and of these few still fewer can use their voices to express it.

At the back of all this bad teaching is a sort of moral notion that education is somehow better for us if it is un-comfortable.   Scholarship must be arduous, and therefore painful.   When English was at last admitted at Oxford as a means to an honours degree, its opponents managed to wedge masses of Anglo-Saxon into the syllabus, not because it helped, but because it was difficult.   They did not want the appreciation of our literature to be a soft option.   (Ask any practising writer or critic, who has spent most of his conscious lifetime in training his responses to life and letters, for a comment on this idea.) The headmaster of the school where I used to teach never ceased to complain that I read to my classes instead of " making them work," and several times burst into the room where they listened in comfortable relaxation and roared at them to sit up straight. Only the fact that my examination results were good enabled him to tolerate my immoral methods at all.

Part of the blame for this lies in the English character, which likes to respond to every stimulus with action. To be up and doing, even if you are not sure what it is or why you are doing it, comes more easily than to sit still and listen. This characteristic accounts for much premature action : and action without sufficient preliminary thought is another name for our traditional policy of muddling through. The magazine short story, all plot and movement, where no one thinks and every problem is solved by action ; the essentially emotional nature of our political and corporate decisions* ; the importance, in English medicine, of prescriptions and advice definite enough to make the patient feel that something is being *done* about his complaint : Kipling's advice to English victims of depression,

> . . . *to take a large hoe*
> *and a shovel or so*
> *and dig till you gently perspire :*

all these are evidence of our ineptitude for repose and for analysis, for consciously listening to the inner voice.

Only when confronted with music do we as a nation relax and listen. In the concert hall we lose our self-consciousness. Then all our craving for action leaves us, and many of our emotional inhibitions go with it. We are deeply responsive to music. Many who would scorn to be moved by verse can unashamedly give themselves up to orchestra

---

* We salve our conscience by holding a full-dress debate on the point at issue, and then make a decision on purely emotional grounds, ignoring all that has been said on either side.

or choir. You can see their spirits in their faces, and, even if they knew you could, they would be past caring.

Is it fanciful to suggest that this is in part because the appeal is to a sense which their English teaching has neglected : to the ear ? Even where it is reasonably well presented, English is in school presented only to the eye. We learn to write it, after a fashion—usually in a way and for a purpose we could never have chosen. We learn to read it, for the wrong reasons and at the wrong time. We do not learn to speak it at all. And, if poetry is read aloud to us, if Shakespeare or Coleridge is allowed to reach our ears in the class-room, how seldom does the voice of the reader match his sensitiveness, how seldom do both match their theme.

I believe we shall get no satisfactory teaching of English till the ear is restored to its proper place as ally of the eye : till English can come in at both gateways : till our speech is worthy of our inheritance. Our voices are good. What is wrong is the way we use and fail to use them.

CHAPTER II

" . . . leave thy vain bibble babble."

M R. J. B. PRIESTLEY in one of his happiest broadcast programmes made the point that a great deal of everyday conversation does not get beyond the making of polite or friendly noises. It is a device for mutual reconnoitring, something that goes on while the participants are getting to know each other. He instanced a conversation between a girl and her prospective mother-in-law. What they said was almost meaningless, but, while they were saying it, they were intuitively sizing each other up and making friends. The conversation signified no more (if the comparison may be allowed) than the preliminary nosings and tail-waggings of two dogs before they celebrate their new-found friendship in a gambol.

Conversation on this level hardly serves the purpose of speech, since the understanding which follows it is due to other causes. Polite and friendly noises are a basis for speech, rather than speech itself. As a race, we are much addicted to the friendly-noises type of conversation, and to other partial uses of our language. Admittedly, the deepest understandings between individuals often do not need expression in words : which is just as well, since a great many of us could not express them. But these are in a minority. There are other, more general contacts : and the very existence of the word " misunderstanding " shows that words do not always succeed in clearly communicating the intention which has prompted them.

We acquire great skill in the interpretation of friendly noises, particularly when they are in our own key. For instance :—

1st YOUNG LADY : Well, I mean—

2nd YOUNG LADY : I *know*, dear.

1st YOUNG LADY : It seems so—sort of—

2nd YOUNG LADY : Yes, *doesn't* it !

1st YOUNG LADY : I mean, she came out of the lib'ry, and stood there—*you* know—sort of looking at me, as if it was any of *her* business, and then she said did I know, *you* know, all sort of, well, just as if *she* was the one, so I looked at her and said, well, after all, I am his secketry.   So she sort of looked—*you* know—

2nd YOUNG LADY : I should think I do.

1st YOUNG LADY : I mean—it seems so—sort of—

2nd YOUNG LADY : *I* know.

I'm sure she does : but it is no thanks to the expressive power of the story.   Her sympathetic intelligence has had to fill in many gaps and attach several different meanings to the same noise.   As a narrator, her friend draws very inadequately upon the resources of the English language.

This unwillingness to draw on our language, the curious colourlessness of our talk, the overworking of a few words, is often shown up in our conversations with those who, even if they are inexpert in their use of English, are at least uninhibited.   Here is a conversation overheard on a bus between Guildford and London.   It occurred between a young lady and an elderly gentleman of foreign extraction, seated side by side.

The occasion was a poster advertising a forthcoming concert.

GENTLEMAN : You like som' music, yess.

LADY : Yes, I do, *awfully*.

GENTLEMAN : Me too very moch I like.   Gonsert, opera, all sort.

LADY : Yes.

GENTLEMAN : Opera here not good.   Gotta travellink, for good opera.

LADY : It used to be awfully good at Covent Garden, didn't it ?

GENTLEMAN: Yess, bot better travellink. Ven I am yonk, I hear moch opera. Caruso. Melba. Patti—ah, Patti !

LADY: She was awfully goodlooking, wasn't she ?

GENTLEMAN: About a forty bust.

(Stupefied silence, during which it was conjectured that the gentleman dealt in ladies' wearing apparel : a conjecture which proved to be correct.)

GENTLEMAN: Shtill is better travellink. Before the war moch am I travellink everyvere.

LADY: How lovely.

GENTLEMAN: Yess. Nineteen hours am I standink in Barcelona.

LADY: How awful for you.

GENTLEMAN: No no you don' unnerstan' very moch I like. Nineteen hours is my *ship* standink. I go . . . Promenade. Make valks.

LADY: Oh, I see.

GENLTEMAN: Tree veeks am I standink in Varsaw.

LADY: Can you speak Polish ?

GENTLEMAN: Yess, all so good than English I spik.

LADY: How awfully clever of you. Isn't it awfully difficult ?

GENTLEMAN: No. Similar like English, mit different shpellinks.

Here, shpellinks and all, the gentleman made a better showing than the lady. Judged by its variety and its power to communicate experience, his English was more expressive than hers.

At the opposite pole from the polite-noises kind of English is the kind which draws freely upon the resources of the language, but for mistaken or unworthy purposes : even, in some cases, in order to resist interpretation, or conceal the fact that nothing is being said. For example :—

(a) Although it would be imprudent to attach undue credence to reports emanating from sources which, by their very nature, do not admit of precise verification, there would seem to be some justification for inferring the existence of a slight tendency towards optimism rather than the reverse in the special area under consideration.

(*b*) QUESTION : Will the Minister consider extending the same privileges to the tin-workers?

ANSWER : The Government is always anxious to safeguard the interests of every section of the community to the fullest extent that is consistent with a planned economy.

Of these (*a*) means that a Civil Servant with a bad ear (-ation, -ation, -ation) is anxious not to commit himself to a positive statement in case he should get into trouble if it proved to be wrong : and (*b*) means, and is intended to mean, nothing at all.

In examples like the following, considerable demands are made upon the English language, but to no good purpose.

(*c*)   SUPER-EPIC

Colossal !   Stupendous ! !   Immense ! ! !   Superb ! ! ! !

A MIRTHQUAKE IN THREE SPASMS !

You'll roar !   You'll yell ! !   You'll split your sides ! ! !
(And/or)

It's Breathtaking ! It's Stunning ! ! It's Eviscerating ! ! !

A palpitating holocaust of passionate love and hate,

Shot with laughter, lit by tropic suns,

Featuring, *etc.*, *etc.* . . .

This again means nothing at all, but conceals a thing it is careful not to say : which is that a lot of money has been sunk in making a film, and the investors do not wish to lose it. The advertisement is, incidentally, a collective insult to the intelligence of the human race : but that is by the way. Its purpose is to persuade.

The next example was until recently one of the routine announcements at a London terminus :—

(*d*) *Will persons meeting friends, and are unable to contact
them, please go to Platform X* . . .

Person yourself, as the charwoman said. Someone has
evidently been tinkering with this. It probably read " and
who are unable," until the purist pointed out that " who
are " was not needed : " who " got struck out, " are " was
left, and none of the ladies who mouthed the result into
the microphone knew or cared that she was talking nonsense.

All these examples degrade and misuse the English
language by delving into it, without taste or knowledge, or
by turning it to serve unworthy uses.

Here is another conversation, also overheard on a bus.
A couple have just got in, quite young ; a husband taking
his wife to hospital. From their conversation it is obvious
that she has been to the same hospital before. She is in
quite good spirits to start with, but every word he says to
her, with the best of intentions, makes matters worse.

SHE : Now then—mind where you put that suitcase.
You're bumping my legs.

HE : Oh ! That won't do, will it. Mustn't send you in
with nothin' *else* wrong. (*Pause*)

SHE : I wonder if there'll be any of the same nurses left.

HE : Remember that pretty little one ? Little dark girl ?

SHE : No. I can't say I do.

HE : Oh go on, yes, you do. You know—the one who
used to bring us the tea. Nice little girl, she was. I
wouldn't mind seeing her again.

SHE : Well, I don't expect you will. They change the
nurses pretty often, I believe.

HE : Pity. I reckon the almoner will be there, though.
You remember her, don't you ? She was that nice and
kind, when you were leaving.

SHE : Oh, well, I wasn't in a condition to appreciate it.
I don't remember anything much, when I was leaving.

HE : Ah. That's the worst of it. You feel so bad when

you get up. Are we getting near? Hadn't you better—

SHE: No, dear. It's a long way yet. Mind that suit-case, you're rubbing it on my stocking.

HE: Sorry. No proper place to put it. It's too big to go up on top.

SHE: Leave it alone, do. Don't go shuffling it about.

HE: All right, all right. (*Pause*) Ah well: one thing, I shall know me way when I come to visit you.

SHE: Yes. You'll come in to-morrow, won't you?

HE: To-morrow? Oh, I don't think quite so soon—you'll hardly be up to seeing me *to-morrow*.

SHE: Oh yes, I shall. I shall be looking forward to it.

HE: Oh well—d'you really think you'll feel equal to it? Remember how low you were feeling last time. You hadn't hardly come round from the ether, not properly. You were feeling that sick.

SHE: I was counting on seeing you, if it's only for a minute.

HE: Mind you, I don't grudge the time. It isn't that. Only I should have thought it would be more sense the day after. More value, like. But of course, if you'd *like* it—

SHE: Yes, I should like it.

HE: Well, then, I'll come. 'Ere—isn't this where we get out?

SHE: No, dear, not yet. Oh, do mind my stockings with that case. Leave it down, dear, do.

HE: No proper place to put it.

SHE: It'll be all right. We haven't got far to go now.

HE: (*sighs*) You know—I been thinking, what will happen when you're away. It's been worryin' me. I mean, suppose the man calls with the coal, and you're not there to let him in—What'll happen? He'll go away again, and we shan't get no coal. It's been worryin' me.

SHE: Oh, you'll have to manage as best you can.

HE: Oh, we'll *manage* all right, don't you fret. But it is a bit of a worry.

SHE : Well, Mrs. 'Iggings will be in mornings.

HE : Yes—but suppose anyone comes in the afternoon ? And then, there's the house. I mean, Mrs. 'Iggings is all very well, but no one could call her thorough. And she *is* a bit of a smasher.

SHE : Oh well, it won't be for long.

HE : I *hope* not.

SHE : What do you mean, you *hope* not ?

HE : Well, of course I hope not. What else d'you expect me to say ?

SHE : The doctor didn't say anything to you he never said to me, did he ?

HE : 'Course he didn't.

SHE : What about when you were showing him out the door ?

HE : Oh—then ! We wasn't talking about you at all. We was talking about the boxing at the Town 'All. Ha ! Quite a good story he told me. He has to be there, see, in case any of 'em get hurt bad. Well, it seems one chap—

SHE : No. I don't want to hear about it. Not now.

HE : Well, you *are* unreasonable.

SHE : I don't want to hear about great men hurting each other, thank you. I shall have enough without hearing about any more.

HE : Asked me what the doctor said, didn't you ?

SHE : Yes, well, I thought it mighta been about me. After all, it's me he'd been to see. And if you'd had any—

HE : Go on. If I'd had any what ?

SHE : Oh, never mind. It doesn't matter.

HE : I don't know what you mean. Hi ! Here we are.

SHE : Oh, Bert ! *Do* keep that case still.

HE : This is where we get out.

SHE : No. It's two stops more. Put the case down.

HE : Nowhere to put it. Not very comfortable, these seats, are they. All right for loving couples, I daresay.

(*The rest of the journey is made in bleak silence.*)

In this the husband's remarks are expressive enough, with the important qualification that they produce the opposite effect to what he intended. He meant to cheer her up. There was obviously a deep intuitive bond between the two. Underneath, they were perfectly at accord. It was the use of words that put them wrong. The correspondence between what the husband meant and what he said, the relation of words to intention was so weak that his words did harm instead of good.

Such a state of things arises from inability to think straight, and from inability to translate feeling into words. All he could get out was the trivial and unseasonable detail which he should have kept back.

When it comes to the tone of voice in which things are said, and the quality of the voice, nothing will do but a gramophone record. If many English people's grasp of the language is weak, so is their control over the voice. They are handicapped in the means of expression, as well as in the medium. The voice that should convey a state of feeling often conveys something even further from it than the words in some of the conversations we have been looking at.

Only a gramophone record could illustrate the harsh voices, the thick voices, the whining voices, the shallow, all-in-the-front-of-the-mouth voices, the far-back-in-the-throat voices, the metallic, the muffled, the splashy voices, the boring, the exasperating voices, the hundred-and-one disorders of speech which come from disability, neglect, from inner or outer strain, from shyness, fear, depression, insecurity, personal difficulties of every kind, bad living conditions—disorders all recognizable, almost all curable, which attest the close connection between voice and character, voice and experience, voice and life itself.

CHAPTER III

" Thy speech betrayeth thee."

NEW TESTAMENT.

THE relationship of voice to personality is delicately balanced, and the balance very easily disturbed.

To illustrate this, may I give you a brief summary of my own experience ? I do so only because I am able to trace the play of inner and outer causes to an extent that would be difficult if not libellous in the case of any one else. If you are not interested, or if you can accept the opening sentence of this chapter, you may skip what follows.

As a child, I was told to shut up in the singing class because I could not sing in tune. I soon established that this was not a defect of ear by teaching myself to play upon a kind of zither. My father had a more than pleasant singing voice, and, when I was little, he used to take me into the drawing-room and sing me Victorian ballads by the hour (afflicting me with a predilection I have never quite outgrown !). I was also struck with admiration of the bass voice of one of our assistant masters at my preparatory school, a Welshman named Rees, and my cup of joy was full when my father heard and praised it.

My father's father had died when he was twelve, obliging him to leave school and start to work. I was in a constant state of anxiety lest I too should have to provide for my mother and sister. There was one thing I thought I might be able to do. I loved the stage, and particularly the music hall, and, being imitative, I could copy the comedians I heard in pantomime and on the halls. They sang raucously : I copied them.

Mimicry had come easy, as we lived on the fringe of Dartmoor, and spent our summer holidays at my grandfather's house near Dublin. I soon had a wide range of accents, and visits to the Abbey Theatre in Dublin made my use of them more conscious. I also got, from Sara Allgood, Fred O'Donovan, and others, my first clear idea of beautiful speaking.

My interest in singing grew. On a half-holiday from school I took myself to a performance of *The Messiah*, and was astounded by the diction and attack of Joseph Farrington, the bass, and the silvery poignancy of Sydney Coltham. Soon after this I heard records of Caruso and McCormack, and realized for the first time the possibilities of the human voice.

At my public school, the Headmaster took us once a week in English. I evidently had a West Country accent, for he made me repeat each week " The third bird never heard a word," which I must have rendered as " The thurd burd nevur hurd a wurd." To what extent he cured me, I don't know.

I sang comic songs at school, developing considerable power on wrong lines, and I began to act. By the time I went up to Oxford I had done quite a lot, in a completely untaught way. We bought a gramophone, I started to collect records, and my musical education began. At Oxford I joined the Music Club, and had among my friends a composer and an organist. The composer one day made me sing. In my alarm I avoided the unpleasant noises I had learned to make, and he concluded that while I had very little voice, what I had was of pleasant if somewhat plaintive quality.

I was now singing a great deal, choosing buffo, character and folk songs, and getting away with them on diction, dialect, and a sense of character. I found I had, somehow, the ability to put a song over to an audience, and this covered the worst of my faults and weaknesses. I was acting rather than singing, and using the power of my wrongly produced voice for comic purposes. I joined a company of amateur actors, and had the privilege of working under Rosina Filippi. She and the company in which I found myself taught me a lot. I played the Ballad Singer in Lady Gregory's *The Rising of the Moon* several times in London, and was advised that it would be worth my while to take singing lessons.

Three or four years passed before I could act on this advice. Then I turned up for my first lesson from the bass singer Frederick Grisewood, since known to millions for his work on the air. Freddie, who had a fine voice of great range, was a former pupil of Victor Beigel, with Gervase Elwes, Hubert Eisdell, John Adams, and many another. It took him a couple of years to undo the harm I had done by bawling my character songs.

While this was going on I was teaching English to the scholarship form of a famous preparatory school. I did a lot of reading aloud in class and, with that queer half-conscious prevision which often inspires us, I slowly taught myself to read aloud.

Round about 1928 I was interviewed at the old B.B.C. headquarters at Savoy Hill by Miss Hilda Matheson, who came to the conclusion that I was totally unsuited to broadcasting. In the same year, thanks to the tuition of Freddie Grisewood and the help of Sir Arnold Bax, I obtained an audition as a baritone singer. I chose an Irish folk song, and diction, brogue, and character got me through. On the same day I was taken before one of the drama producers, read him a passage from *The Playboy of the Western World*, and was offered a part in a forthcoming broadcast of an Irish play : but I could not get away from Oxford for rehearsals, and had sorrowfully to refuse. I followed this up by singing under a pseudonym in a London restaurant : that, with two more microphone efforts, being the sum total of my singing career.

Now, at last, you will see the point of all this. I began broadcasting in 1933. A record was made of one broadcast, and I was invited to listen. It was one of the most terrible shocks I have ever had.

The voice was thin, nasal, deprecating, and pitched in a minor key. It was a hotchpotch of accents : Dublin (a little), Devon (a lot), with a disgusting overlay of Oxford not out of the top Oxford drawer. Its range was small. Only in dialect had it any freedom.

I did my best to improve. In 1936 I acceded at last to my old friend Richard Church's repeated request to come and judge at the annual Oxford Festival of Spoken Verse. While I was still an undergraduate, I had heard John Drinkwater read verse, and had been astonished by the beauty of his performance. None of the other poets whom I knew, Yeats, A.E., and others, could approach him in the combination of a poet's ear and a trained voice. I did not want to hear anything less good : so I had fought shy of the Festival.

I was instantly converted. For the first time I realized what good speaking can do for verse. A great deal of the speaking we heard was bad, insensitive, tricky, full of sense-emphasis, which destroyed the music of the verse, and generally what that admirable comedian Mr. Teddy Knox once described as " fandandicated." But every now and then came the miracle of beautiful speaking : and it was a revelation.

It shouldn't have been. When I had listened to Sara Allgood, Frank Fay, and the others, the fact that they spoke with an Irish accent seemed to set their work apart. And, except on a single occasion, I had not heard any of them speak lyric verse. Drinkwater's speaking likewise seemed exceptional. Now for the first time I heard a series of speakers use the English language beautifully and give to the poems a new dimension. And, I repeat, it was a revelation. That it was, indicts the whole of my so-called education in English. Drinkwater's reading no longer seemed a special dispensation : I saw that the power to speak verse well was in the power of everyone with an ear and a voice which was under control.

After more judging, I began to examine in the University of London's Diploma in Dramatic Art. Since one cannot help students without knowing their difficulties, I began to speak verse myself, on platforms and over the air. My voice was still very unsatisfactory. I had come to some sort of terms with the microphone as a solo reader, but a programme shared with the actors Lewis Casson and Hubert Gregg proved me miserably inadequate. I consulted two actor friends, and was sent to a teacher of genius, whom I already knew but had not ventured to consult— Miss Gwynneth Thurburn, now Principal of the Central School of Speech Training and Dramatic Art.

By the time I went to her, I had discovered something. When I spoke in my own person, my voice was poor and thin, with a plaintive minor tone. When I spoke in dialect, Dublin or Devon, there was a seventy per cent. improvement. I read a speech from Synge's *Playboy* to Miss Thurburn, so that she might hear the difference. In three lessons, she did more for me than all the rest of my work put together. She showed that unsureness of myself, unsureness of the worth of what I had to say, inhibited my voice when I spoke in my own person. It caused certain muscles to contract, sending my voice up into my head above its normal pitch. I understood why B.B.C. producers at first had always urged me to " speak down." I understood, too, why one of them came in during a rehearsal and said, " Yes, now, we all know you're a nice modest little chap. Forget it, and for God's sake get some self-assertion into your voice."

And I understood a complementary fact. At home, as a child, I was taken great care of, and had to mind my p's and q's. But when I got away to a neighbouring farm, I might get my feet wet and do as I pleased. *On the farm, everyone spoke Devon dialect*.

Similarly, in my grandfather's Irish garden I was safely enclosed and lovingly looked after. But down on the Sea

Wall, with my fishermen friends, I could relax and be a normal little boy. *My fishermen friends spoke Dublin dialect.*

Thus these two dialects had become for me the symbols of freedom, and in using them my voice lost its tension and became something like the voice Nature meant me to have. Miss Thurburn gave me a few simple technical exercises, and my voice soon improved in range and freedom.

Then, just as I was feeling more or less happy, came a fierce test. I was engaged to write and compère a series of programmes starring Count John McCormack. I had learned to work close to the microphone, and so could avoid comparative disadvantage even in broadcasts with actors. Here, however, I had to work in a large studio with an orchestra and a variety of speakers. If I spoke confidentially into the microphone, they would get no lead, I would depress them, there would be no attack to the various sections of the programme. And I had to stand up to my principal and exchange backchat with him—he with a speaking voice no less expressive, and more powerful, than his singing voice.

At the first broadcast with him I was so bad he wished aloud and in my presence that he could get rid of me : but for the remaining five I managed well enough to satisfy and even to please him, a fact which, with his characteristic generosity, he did not hesitate to proclaim.

I still have difficulties, I still hear a great deal that I dislike in my voice. I do not speak standard English, and never shall ; but that is by the way. Only by hard work and a period of deliberate preparation can I get my voice to do what I want of it, and express me as I am.

Now : it will be apparent that the greater part of the training I have received and the work I have done was spent in unlearning bad habits and undoing the harm done by working on the wrong lines. It will be apparent, too, that a lot of my faults arose from anxiety, self-distrust, and other inner causes. I must have some native ability, or I could not have done anything at all, and I would not be able to earn with my voice the money I do.

But—if only there had been someone at school to show me how to use my voice properly ! If only there had been someone to get rid of those dead unresonant vowels, those false intonations ! To stop me from singing in my throat and achieving volume by tightening instead of by relaxing !

If only there had been someone to read verse and prose really well ! If only there had been someone to give me confidence to be myself, and so get rid of that diffident minor key !

And, when the way a child speaks has even deeper effects upon self-confidence ; when it threatens his sense of social security ; when he has a physical speech defect which gets in his way ; when he has a voice which puts other people off, and misleads them as to what he is really like inside : how much greater is the need. Yet we still teach English through the eye. We still leave children to pick up their speaking of it haphazard, as best they can. We still withhold from them the help we are only beginning to realize they need and we can give.

You will have seen from my history how deeply voice is bound up with character and experience, how sensitive is the balance and the harmony between the psychological and physical aspects of speech. If I have made these points clear, this chapter will have done what I wanted.

CHAPTER IV

" He was deeply hurt, not only in his feelings, but in those depths where the physical, the emotional and the spiritual roots of existence are inextricably interwoven."

DEMETRIOS CAPETANAKIS' ESSAY ON DOSTOEVSKY.

THE way a person speaks is bound up closely with his inner life, influencing it and influenced by it. Any teacher of speech will confirm this. The progress of students is often held up by emotional difficulties ; and, when these difficulties are eased or removed, the voice can respond in a way that seems miraculous.

The range of disturbance is from tension and hardness of tone to positive speech defect. It can be collective, as on one occasion in my experience, when at a competition all the competitors' voices were tight and hard in tone, as the reslut of nervous tension caused by a row behind the scenes.

Individual disturbances are legion. A student whose home life was cramped by possessive and anxious parents was unable for years to achieve real freedom of tone. A girl of eleven was unable to pronounce the letter B : it was discovered that her younger sister had supplanted her in her mother's affection ; the younger sister's name began with B : and the sufferer, though quite unable to say " Bless Betty " at the therapist's suggestion, responded explosively to the command to say " Blast Betty "—showing that the disability was altogether of psychological origin. The voice of a contralto speaker rose three semi-tones and lost all its natural colour during a period of nervous stress. It would be easy to fill a book with instances of the relation of vocal to emotional tone and the interaction between speech and inner life.

But more than the inner life is concerned. It is difficult

to exaggerate the practical importance of clear and accurate and pleasant speaking, in ordinary, everyday intercourse. Socially and economically the individual's progress and welfare depend to an increasing extent upon the way he speaks.

The vast majority of human beings judge a person superficially, by externals. What does he or she look like? How does he or she dress? That is about as far as they go in the category of appearances. The exterior offered confidently or shrinkingly is accepted : few trouble to probe beneath it.

The other external token is speech. How does he or she speak? And only in cases where it is very noticeably pleasant or unpleasant—what sort of voice has he or she got? Many a pretty girl is made unattractive by a harsh or metallic voice. Many a good-looking man sounds boring or otherwise intolerable because his voice is unpleasing or monotonous. I know of at least one divorce of which the sole cause was the irritation of an unmusical voice upon a sensitive ear. I have seen a candidate for a good post rejected at an interview because, although his qualifications were excellent, he had a pompous way of speaking.

The quest of " golden voices " for telephone girls : the failure of so many stars of the silent screen when talkies came along : the affection in which certain radio announcers are held : sensitiveness of children to the tone of adult speech : all these are indications of the great importance which people attach, even if unnecessarily, to the quality of the speaking voice.

" She's lovely till she opens her mouth."

" Yes, it was a good lecture, but I found it terribly hard to listen to."

" His speeches read well, but his voice makes everything he says sound insincere."

"She's got such a *sympathetic* voice I could listen to her all night."

We are continually hearing this kind of thing : and it is
not new.   Lear proclaimed it :—

> *Her voice was ever soft,*
> *Gentle and low, an excellent thing in woman.*

Even more important than its quality is the way the voice
is used.   Apart from the often considerable problem of
understanding what is said, the chief ground for deciding
differences of social status is the way we speak.   I would go
so far as to say that real democracy is impossible as long as
differences in speaking are held to connote differences in
social position.   As long as certain ways of speech are
regarded as base, and those who have acquired them in early
childhood are given no regular, matter-of-course opportunity to correct or supersede them, then democracy will be
little more than a form.   Equality of franchise, yes.
Equality of opportunity, never, so long as to speak in a
certain way is automatically to be debarred from some of
the best opportunities.

Moreover, the importance of the spoken word is steadily
increasing.   The written word no longer predominates.
The widespread use of the telephone, the growing power
of radio, the improvement in communications, are all
making clear and intelligible speech a necessity.   Intelligible
speech : speech that can be understood and accepted at
once, without difficulty, and without making the hearer
start speculating to the speaker's disadvantage : speech that
persuades, or at least does not arouse antagonism, thereby
wasting time and imperilling communications : this is no
longer a luxury.   Modern life cannot do without it.

The question goes far beyond dialect, of which I shall
have plenty to say presently.   We are brought up against
problems of ordinary efficiency.   It was found necessary in
the R.A.F. to employ speech teachers in order that a bomb-
aimer from Wolverhampton and his colleague from Devonport might understand each other's excited instructions over
the inter-com.   A boy or girl from the West Riding may

fail to get a post in a London circulating library, not because
its patrons have any prejudice against Yorkshire speech, but
because they cannot understand it. Add a mechanical defect of voice or speech, and you have a serious economic and
social handicap—and one that is quite unnecessary.

*Most defects of voice and all defects of accent are curable : and
the earlier the cure is undertaken the better are its chances of a
complete success.*

How long, for want of qualified teaching, are we going
to allow these hindrances to remain ? How long are we
going to weaken the root idea of democracy by failing to
remove one of its worst enemies ? How long are we going
to let children grow up and go out into the world maimed ?
For the person whose voice and way of speaking do not
express him, but are merely the result of environment,
uncorrected, unhelped, allowed to become inveterate, is
maimed in the all-important matter of his relation to his
fellow-beings. He had better in many cases be a cripple :
it will hinder him less.

This fact is recognized when the child has a definite
physical or functional speech defect, a cleft palate, a stammer,
an inability to sound this or that letter. Most education
authorities nowadays employ a qualified speech therapist.
But training of the normal voice is still the exception. Bad
tone, clipped vowels, base inflections ; voices harsh, muffled,
strained, over-loud, breathy, thick, unmodulated, inexpres-
sive ; voices that can give neither a true picture of personality nor an even reasonably adequate rendering of the
English tongue : these get no treatment. It does not seem
to have occurred to anyone that they need it.

The Norwood Report did some disservice to the cause of
Spoken English by the unfortunate wording of one of its
recommendations. It appeared to decry the work of the
qualified teacher of speech, in insisting that every teacher
was a teacher of English. In the sense that he is a teacher,
and uses English, this of course is true. But the implied

idea that the work may be left to him, and that, however
well he himself may speak, he is therefore qualified to teach
his pupils how to speak, is grotesquely untrue.   The Committee seem to have laboured in the belief that a trained
teacher will teach an affected, precious manner of speaking.
Only an untrained or mis-trained speaker could do this.

*The aim of the trained teacher is and must always be to free the
natural voice, and enable its possessor to use it with confidence,
ease, and freedom.*

What the Norwood Committee may have intended to
say was that every teacher of English ought to be a good
example of how to speak it.   It should be impossible to get
a post as English specialist without a course of training in
speaking and reading aloud.   If that was the Committee's
intention, I agree most heartily : but I have no use at all
for this amateurish, let's-all-muddle-along-like-little-ladies-
and-gentlemen attitude to the very important question of
clear speaking.   One can see perfectly well where it comes
from.   The world is full of so-called elocutionists who
speak abominably, and mislead their pupils.   But the day
of these miscreants is past.   The training available to-day
at any of the recognized Schools and Centres does not produce, but ruthlessly suppresses, these monstrosities and
diseases of speech.   If only the doubters could be persuaded
to come and hear examples of good speaking, to visit a
School and hear it at work, they would speedily lose their
fears.

The prejudice against training is real, in so far as it re-
mains a prejudice.   There are still people who will tell you
that training spoils the singing voice.   Bad training spoils
any voice : but the untrained singer will not get far.   There
are English singers living whose voices were of world
quality, but who never got beyond England because they
were not properly trained.   The strain of keeping a balance
with orchestra or choir was wrongly met, and even genius
could not avert the results.

The same is true of speaking. How many actors and actresses come after a few years to have their strained and damaged voices patched by the skilled teachers they should have had before they were allowed on the stage at all. How many voices never realize their natural beauty because they cannot make without distortion the effort demanded by large audiences and difficult halls.

In 1944 Mr. Stephen Potter, looking for speakers of verse for the B.B.C., gave auditions to three hundred and fifty untrained voices, recommended to him from all parts of the country. *Of the three hundred and fifty he was able to use only one :* not, be it remembered, for speaking on a platform or in a large hall, but for the natural intimate speech and unforced volume asked for by the microphone.

Another B.B.C. producer, who cherished a prejudice against the trained voice, discovered an untrained girl with a voice of great natural beauty, and a simple and sensitive manner of reading verse. The rehearsal was perfect, but the broadcast was a fiasco, for the simple reason that the speaker, not knowing how she got her effects, was unable to reproduce them to order. She could not repeat deliberately the performance she had given spontaneously at rehearsal.

It will be objected that only a very small proportion of people need or wish to speak verse in public. True : but the first requisite for speaking verse is the ability to use one's voice naturally, with that added control which only consciousness can bring. To have one's voice under control means that whatever one may be feeling is expressed in the voice directly and spontaneously. A voice choked or muted with feeling expresses nothing. Feeling tends to inhibit speech rather than to inspire it. This may not matter in the sphere of private conversation, but the teacher reading aloud to the class, the parent telling a story to the children, the debater, the barrister, the amateur actor, the preacher, must not allow feeling to get in the way of what they have to say. Those whom occasion or duty calls on to communicate their feeling to others must be able to do so : and the first step is some degree of control over the voice.

No less useful, no less necessary, is the power to speak so that the foreigner may understand us. This point needs no emphasizing. Anyone who has had to lecture to audiences whose knowledge of English is imperfect can bear witness that this is a job which calls for exceptional clarity of speech, purity of pronunciation, and variety of pitch and pace : in a word, for real control of the organs of speech. But ordinary conversation makes demands enough. Sympathy goes only part of the way. We must be able to make it effective.

I remember reading in the last war of the *impasse* between a Belgian refugee and the proprietor of a village shop in Devon, as reported wonderingly by the latter.

" ' Ow much ? ' her saith. ' Shul'n'apmy (a shilling and a halfpenny)', I says. ' Shul'n'apmy,' I says again, so clear's clear. I fair bawls it an' 'olleys it into 'er 'earole. ' Shul'n'-apmy,' I says—but do you think I could make 'er understand ? Not a bit o't."

Here perhaps there was a fundamental failure in sympathy : but the moral is plain. Unless we can use our own language with reasonable freedom and clearness of expression—and, no less important, unless our voice reflects clearly our intention and the quality of our feeling—we cannot effectively communicate with anyone whose idiom is different from our own.

The celebrated Yorkshire conversation between the commercial traveller and the tradesman :

C.T. : " Owt ? "

T. : " Nowt."

(*exit* C.T.)

is beautifully expressive to those who know the idiom, but cryptic to the stranger.

CHAPTER V

" Wot I liked about that party was, they was all of
'em so ree-fined." MUSIC-HALL SONG.

THIS brings us to the disputed question of " Standard
English."

What is the best form of English ? Why ? Who speaks
it ? To what extent should those who do not speak it try
to copy it ?

Each of these questions is certain to rouse strong feelings
and set tongues violently to work. Claims to speak the
best English will be received from educated circles in
Dublin and Edinburgh. The industrial North will stoutly
prefer its lengthened u in words like *fun* and *bucket* (u pro-
nounced as Southerners sound it in *pudding*) and its pro-
pensity to sound the g twice in the middle of words like
springing. Oxford and the West Highlands will each
manage to convey a sense of superiority. Certain of the
Dominions will have their own views, as will the U.S.A.
The inhabitants of the Home Counties will complacently
point to the fact that, for practical purposes, on the air, on
the stage, and wherever English speaking is taught,
" Standard Received English " is that spoken in the South.
The accent of the B.B.C. announcer politely but inexorably
sets the tone.

The fact is bitterly resented, especially in the outspoken
and independent North. There are many who see in it a
deliberate attempt to drag in a public utility company on
the side of class distinctions and social inequality. Others
complain that the tone of the announcers is too impersonal
and lacks character, that the mechanization involved in
transmitting speech has spread to speech itself. A further
section finds the speaking pedantic and over-articulated.
Individualists protest that it is yet another symptom of the
drive towards a soulless uniformity. Dominions listeners

29

have objected to some of it that it is lacking in manliness. In a word, there has been in many places and for various reasons a repudiation of it as the standard to be aimed at.

Before we discuss the question of Standard English, I would like to say a word about the announcers. Their function and difficulties are widely misunderstood, as is the policy of the B.B.C. in choosing them. First of all, their alleged impersonal tone. I often get letters from listeners asking why the news cannot be read with the warmth, the conviction and charm of broadcasters such as Mr. Desmond MacCarthy, Commander Anthony Kimmins, and others equally famous for the degree of intimacy and personal integrity which their voices convey.

The answer is very simple. These men are talking of their own accord on subjects of their own choice, about which they feel strongly. Moreover, they do not talk about them very often. The announcer, on the other hand, has to talk very often on subjects in which his degree of interest must vary very greatly. Some of them may interest him deeply. On others he will be quite indifferent. If he were to allow the degree of his interest to appear in his voice, listeners whose degree of interest differed would soon object. If he becomes excited over a news item, protests come in from all over the country. If his inflection seems sarcastic, flippant, depressed, jaunty, vicious, indifferent, what you will, those who feel strongly about the item in question will have a lot to say. The announcer can't please everybody. But, unlike the occasional broadcaster, whose first need is a clear-cut personality, directly and sincerely expressed, which listeners take or leave, the announcer must try to please as many listeners as possible. They have got to listen to him, if they want to hear the news, and other items of importance to them : so, even by the negative method of trying to displease as few people as possible, he has to make the attempt. He has to be inoffensive, or as inoffensive as he can. So he plays for safety, aiming at a smooth clarity of tone which shall dissociate him, as far as is humanly possible, from the matter he has to announce. (I am thinking now chiefly of the news. The announcers of variety programmes, etc., simulate eagerness and enthusiasm, in order to tone in with the occasion.)

As a race, we grumble at anything which is given us : but we very positively dislike the jocular, two-handed-punching style of announcing, sometimes favoured in other quarters.

" Say, folks, who d'you think we got in the studio to-night ? If it ain't Sir—Adrian—Boult and the B.B.C. Symphony Orchestra, just itchin' to dish out Beethoven's Seventh Symphony. Ready, boys ? Let her go ! "

We should not like this sort of thing. We should prefer impersonality.

Besides, for his own protection the announcer must aim at a non-committal efficiency. He has not only to be everybody's friend, to make himself acceptable to all ; he has to achieve a manner of presenting what he has to say which will do justice to all of it. The personality of each announcer is distinct. Voice being so closely bound up with personality, he cannot keep personality out. But, in contrast to the ordinary broadcaster, his business is to keep it in the background : to be the voice of the B.B.C. rather than of the individual.

And, on the whole, he does his job very well. Stand any broadcaster up to the test of regular exposure to the great mass of the listening public, and see how he fares ! Experienced broadcasters have the greatest respect for these regular voices of the B.B.C. They know the hash *they* would make of the job, if ever they had to try it. These well-trained voices—most announcers are or have been singers or actors—have achieved a wonderful level of clear and intelligent and pointed speech, in conditions which are far from easy : and we owe a great deal to them.

Most of the same considerations govern the choice of

Southern English as the medium in which the news, etc., is presented.   Its advantages are these :—

(*a*) It is immediately understood by the majority of English-speaking people.

(*b*) It offends fewer people than any other form of English.

(*c*) It is more easily understood abroad than any other form of English.   Being " Standard English", it is what foreigners are taught.   Except in very special cases, to confront them with a provincial accent would confuse and bewilder them.

These considerations do not appease the susceptibilities of large sections of the population where other forms of English are used.   They demand that their way of speaking should be at least represented : that one announcer should speak Lowland Scottish, another Yorkshire, another West Country, and so on.

I sympathize strongly : but I feel that the place for such announcers is in the Regional Stations.   The first requisite of news readers is that they should be heard and understood without difficulty by the greatest possible number of listeners. A Bradford or a Glasgow or a Plymouth accent is less widely understood than Standard English.   That argument seems to me final.   I hate uniformity, I love diversity of accent and phrase, but the purpose of announcing is utilitarian rather than picturesque.   Standard English has it over all competitors.   Judged by strictly academic rules, I don't speak it myself, although I come close enough to it to be understood in any part of the country I have visited : but then, I'm not an announcer.   If I were, every smallest variation from Standard English would be a drawback and would hamper my work.

Now for the larger question.   Why should Southern English be taken as Standard ?   Why should we copy it ?

The range of English dialect is so wide, and the dialects are so different, that nobody can be expected to master them all.   Having heard a Devonian and a Dubliner try to converse, I can bear witness that each was speaking what was to the other a foreign language. A Devonian and a Yorkshireman fared no better. *Some* form of English must be taken as Standard. There are standards in French, Italian, Spanish, in every language. Usually, for obvious reasons, the standard will be the speech of educated people in the capital city. That is what has happened with us (and it leads to the regrettable corollary that the uneducated speech of the capital is regarded as the least desirable of the dialects).

That this should be so is doubtless an affront to the civic pride of the Northerner : but a greater number of people are suited by the establishment of Southern English as Standard. It is the speech of educated people in almost every part of Britain. (The natives of Edinburgh, Manchester, etc., etc., are often anxious to shed all trace of local accent.) In form and phrasing it corresponds more nearly to written English. Everyone can understand it.

Why should we copy it ? Well, no one compels us to. It's a free country. But there are several reasons why, in our own interest, we should be able to do so if we wish.

It is difficult to discuss this question without sounding snobbish, but it can be done, as I learned once for all at a conference in the West Country. The occasion was a refresher course for teachers of English from Elementary Schools. I had been talking about broadcasting, and the inevitable question of Standard English arose.

I said what I have always felt and believed, that dialect enriched the language and should on no account be lost. A man who was ashamed of his native accent was as bad as a man who was ashamed of his home and his parents. But he should have at his command a universal as well as a local English. He needs a *lingua franca*, something which will be acceptable and intelligible wherever he goes. He should be able to speak, or at any rate to imitate, Standard English.

" Let's be realists," I said. " Let's face the facts. It's wrong, it's unreasonable, it's indefensible, but the hard fact is that certain local accents are considered pleasant and socially presentable, and others are not. You will be allowed to have a Scottish colour to your voice, but not a Cockney. You may talk Cardiff, but not Devonport—and so on and so forth. To talk with certain accents is a social and economic handicap. It ought not to be, but it is."

There followed a few minutes of heated discussion, and then a youngish man got up. In excellent Standard English he informed us that to speak broad Devon, as he was brought up to do, was a hindrance in any part of the country but Devon. He had therefore had himself taught Standard English, since when his progress had been good and promised to be even better. What was more, he had lost his sense of inferiority which his accent had given him outside his home.

" You abm lost yer Debm, I'll lay," I interjected.

" Git ome with ee, man," he replied. " Wat dee take me for ? 'Course I abm."

His contribution eased any tension there may have been in the room. The company grinned, and relaxed in their chairs.

" The world being as it is," I put it to them, " and it being our duty as teachers to equip our pupils to make their way in it, are we justified in exposing them to the additional difficulty of not being able to speak in a way that will be acceptable wherever they go ? Ought we to leave them suffering from the sense of inferiority they won't be able to help, if they feel they can't speak ' like other people ' ? They feel insecure enough as it is. Why add to their burden ? "

I was examining once with John Laurie, the actor, at a well-known stage school in London. One very promising boy actor spoke with clipped vowels and bad diphthongs (" heouse " for house, etc.). John Laurie pulled him up.

" Listen," he said. " I know you can't hear that sound in your own voice, any more than I can hear that I have a Scottish accent. Mine seems natural to me, and yours seems natural to you. But you're at the age when it can be very easily put right. It's a personal matter, I know, but you mustn't mind my telling you about it. If no one does tell you, you'll go out into the world, and sooner or later you'll be told of it. Maybe you'll lose a part because of it, a big part which you very much want. Then you'll say ' I was at the Such-and-such School. Why didn't they tell me ? ' Well—I'm telling you now."

Print will not reproduce the kindliness and good-humour with which the words were spoken : but I don't see how one could improve on them as a statement of the case for teaching Standard English in our schools.

It is, I repeat, quite indefensible that one native way of speaking should be a social handicap and another an advantage. It has nothing to do with the quality of the speech as speech. A Hampshire or a Warwickshire rustic speaks far better than many a Mayfair young lady : but his broad and open vowels and his burred r's are held to signify lack of education, while her clipped and slovenly speech—she pinches her o's, calls a war a waw, pronounces beer as beah, gets her books from the lahbry, and, 'v cawce, lives in Mayfah—hers is in some circles the social passport to Paradise. Ask any teacher which of the two he'd rather teach. Contrast the vocal health of one with the other. Compare the use they make of their respective opportunities. The rustic will learn to speak good English far sooner than she.

That is the whole point. Standard English is easily acquired. I sometimes visit schools to which (among others) are sent the daughters of North Country and Midland business men, to acquire this way of speaking. They soon acquire it. A teacher who knows the job gets very quick results.

Admittedly, the additional manner (I have, I hope, made it clear that I regard it always as additional, and would wish no one to forgo his or her home accent when at home), the

additional manner has to be learned, at first, as a thing apart.
There are very many singers who sing beautiful Standard
English, but speak with broad accents in everyday conversation. They have learned the Standard English, of
necessity, for professional purposes. So can we all learn to
speak it, and acquire the extra self-confidence, the social and
commercial advantage, the extra freedom which it brings.

In the world as it is, the world we have to live in, to
speak Standard English does bring freedom and advantages.
And the sooner we start to learn, the easier it is.

I, as I said before, have learned to speak a pretty close
approximation to Standard English. But I was never
taught. My Headmaster's rough-and-ready effort to correct
my burred Devonian r's was the only teaching I received—
till the three lessons referred to in Chapter III; and they
were for the production of the voice, not for pronunciation.
I had to pick up speaking as best I could. Being something of a mimic, and having had the chance to hear my
voice on gramophone records, I have been able to make a
reasonable shot at it.

To sum up: I am all for the retention of dialect and
local accent, but would stress the desirability of our being
able also to speak an English which anyone can accept and
understand. A few accents are intrinsically bad, because
they come from unnatural conditions. Some forms of
Cockney, the Glasgow glottal stop, the Dublin snuffle, are
the result of physical defects caused by slum living. They
are diseases of speech, just as much as stammering and the
sounds produced by a cleft palate. But all natural and
healthy accents and dialects and idioms are good, and
should be kept.

We should treat the problem as a practical one. We
should learn Standard English for its usefulness and for the
power it will give us. Learn it, and help to make the idea
of democracy real. Once we can all speak it, none of us
can throw stones.

CHAPTER VI

" I had rather the Town Crier spoke my lines."

HAMLET.

OF course, there are other reasons for learning Standard English besides considerations of social and commercial advantage. I have put these first because the whole intention of those in charge of education in this country is that every child should have the chances to which his powers entitle him. His powers, not the amount of money his father has. Any two children of equal ability should have equal chances. That is the intention—and it cannot be fulfilled as long as one of them speaks in a way which hampers his progress, and is not taught to get rid of his handicap.

But there are other considerations. When well spoken, Standard English represents the language at its most beautiful. The speaking of Forbes Robertson, Henry Ainley, Robert Speaight, and other exceptional voices gives to English its inherent quality. Standard English is no rigid thing. It is, by and large, the speech of educated speakers of English. Bernard Shaw's very beautiful speaking voice has its trace of Dublin, but only as a variation, the degree of personal idiosyncrasy which the language loves. The late Lord Hewart's forensic utterances had traces of his native place, but was none the less a model in its kind. The precisely modulated tones of Viscount Simon, the fine resonance of Sir Stafford Cripps, the noble tones with which Dr. C. A. Alington was wont to fill Eton Chapel : these are all examples of the strength and variety of Standard English. The Dean of St. Paul's, Dr. Matthews, the Rev. W. H. Elliott, and many another likewise attest its weight and dignity.

If I have mentioned only men, it is because women as a

rule speak so much better that to choose names would be invidious. They do not always speak well: the worst speakers I have heard have all been women: but their average is far better than the men's. At every festival and competition I have ever attended, the men have had to be judged by a lower standard than the women. This may be partly because more girls are taught to use their voices, girls' schools having realized this important part of their responsibility sooner than boys'; but it is an undoubted fact. I can think of three or four women beautiful speakers for every man.

At festivals and competitions, of course, it is formal speech that we are considering, not ordinary conversation. Not everyone has any desire to speak from the platform, or to speak formally at all: but everyone should be *able* to do so. Learning to speak formally is the best correction for those drawbacks of voice and speech we have been talking about. Just as a stammerer can very often sing clearly and without difficulty, once the additional effort frees him from his disability, so the speaker whose voice is imprisoned or whose articulation is bad is enabled to lose these hindrances in the attempt to speak formally. The rhythms of verse or the discipline of playing a part can bring about a release from difficulties which hitherto have cramped all self-expression through speech. I can think of nobody who would not benefit by training in formal speech, that is, speech as performance: and, except for the playing of character parts in plays, nine-tenths of formal speech is standard English.

A well-trained voice is unobtrusive, it sounds natural, it does not draw attention to the difficulties which it surmounts. That great singer, Sir George Henschel, who kept his voice into advanced age, singing so well at seventy-eight that foreign impresarios attempted to engage him in the belief that he was a young man, remarks in his memoirs that singing which parades its skill is bad singing. The

same is true of speaking. The dreadful effects of the
e-loc-ew-tion-isssts were no more than an ignorant exaggeration of the mechanics of articulate speech. They were
rank bad speakers. Any speaking which consciously draws
attention to itself is bad. The aim of speech is to express
and communicate. It is the thing spoken which is important. The function of the voice is to speak it as clearly, as
effectively, as beautifully, as possible, so that its full value
may appear. The voice should be always at the service of
the thing to be said.

It is a matter of common experience that the best training
for formal speech, apart from the many technical exercises
towards purity of vowel tone and clear articulation, is the
speaking of verse.

At this point two objections may arise, each from a
different quarter.

(a) " I have no use for poetry, or verse, or whatever you
like to call it. I think it artificial and unnatural. Besides,
I don't like it. To try to learn speaking by means of it
would embarrass me and make my speaking artificial
instead of natural."

(b) " Poetry means a very great deal to me, and I look
on it as sacrilege to use it as a *means* to anything. To treat
poems as mere practice for the voice seems to me a sort of
blasphemy."

The first objection tends to disappear in actual practice.
It is theoretical, a beginner's objection. No students in my
experience, whatever their views on poetry in the abstract,
have ever jibbed at speaking verse once a certain degree of
training had shown them that they could speak it effectively.
Once they discover that rhythm helps them to speak, any
objection to verse as a medium of expression disappears.
For nobody is unaffected by rhythm. An excellent leading
article in *The Times Educational Supplement*, discussing the
teaching of English in schools, insisted that poetry be read
aloud to quite small children. Whether they understood

the meaning of the words was of small importance. What mattered was that they should enjoy the rhythm, and, if they wanted, dance to it.

The childish delight in rhythm is often overlaid in adolescence by self-consciousness, but it is seldom deeply buried. The student who would not read a poem aloud to himself or herself in private will often unconsciously welcome the release of being obliged to do it as part of a lesson, and the voice will benefit greatly by the release. Any teaching of English which neglects the ear is losing more than half the battle. Our English teaching has been not so much blind leaders of the blind as deaf leaders of the deaf.

After all, why shouldn't we enjoy rhythm in verse ? We try to. Even our school teaching doesn't altogether kill it. It only succeeds in preventing us from taking it seriously. We enjoy it in humorous verse. The limerick is still one of the best-liked mediums for bawdy jokes. As a race, we adore Gilbert and Sullivan. What is there odd, or unmanly, or eccentric, or highbrow, in enjoying rhythm in verse ? In delighting to hear a voice respond to it and give to rhythmical words their true music ? Music—we listen to that unashamed. Why not to the music of words ? Nothing but an arid and joyless education has robbed us of this vital part of our birthright. No one spoke verse to us. If we studied Shakespeare, it was through a pedant's filter. If we heard the plays in the theatre, too often the lines were spoken by journeymen whose one concern was to hide the embarrassing fact that the man had written in verse, and who therefore broke the lines up, gutted them of their rhythm, and lost half the dramatic effect of the scene. Yes, the *dramatic* effect. The world's supreme dramatist was not such a fool as to write scene after scene of powerful and tender and magnificent verse if prose would have served as well.

It is this accursed self-consciousness we have got to get rid of, if we are to learn to speak well : and the best place to start is in the school. Small children speak verse with such rigid insistence on the beat that they lose half its beauty and almost all its sense. Never mind : they have hold of the right end of the stick. Soon they can learn to loosen their grasp a little, and let the variety of the lines emerge, the sense, the rhythm rather than the metre. This is soon learned : and the best way to learn is to hear someone speak who can speak. That someone should be the teacher.

It does not matter how many times in the course of this book I repeat that nobody should be allowed to teach English who cannot speak it well enough to give to prose and verse a measure of their native beauty. That is the aim. It is in that sense, *pace* the Norwood or any other Committee, that every teacher should be a teacher of English. *Every* teacher should be able to speak well, and the English specialist supremely well. It is not impossible, given a training which removes defects and hindrances, and releases the voice which is the natural woman or man. Really ugly voices are rare : and even they can be taught to speak good English.

To this training, practice in speaking verse, if not essential (and I should say it is, especially for the teacher), is of the greatest value. It imposes a strict discipline on mind and voice. Practice in it helps the speaking of prose. It raises a host of problems which are not only fascinating, but make one realize how much there is to the speaking of even a simple poem. It demands and encourages deep breathing and control of breath. And, by focusing attention on the words themselves, rather than the tone in which they are spoken, it opens up new possibilities in the communication of meaning and emotion.

And, remember, it is a natural form of art. The earliest story-tellers told their stories in rhymed or rhythmic verse, often to the accompaniment of music. We have kept the music and forgotten the words that went with it. We flock

to hear the orchestra or the choir, and turn our back shame-
facedly on the poem. Our ancestors were wiser, and
nearer to Nature : nearer to childhood. Let us give back
to our children this lost ingredient, which they take so
readily.

To the first objection, then, that a person to whom poetry
says nothing cannot benefit by speaking it aloud, I reply
that only experience can prove or disprove this, and that it
almost invariably disproves it. The second of the two
objections, that it is sacrilegious to use poetry in order to
benefit the voice, will be considered in the next chapter.

CHAPTER VII

*" What we call laws are tentative generalities drawn
from the contemplation of particular works of art."*

LORD DAVID CECIL : "HARDY THE NOVELIST."

ONE of the many reasons why the speaking of verse is
such an excellent training is that there is a great deal
of controversy as to how it should be done. Few things
are better for the expanding mind than the discovery that,
in art at any rate, the certainties are few.

For many reasons, this is a discovery the young are
reluctant to make. When I was teaching, I remember a
very gifted boy of eleven coming up and asking how to
express something in Latin.

" Well," I said, " you can do it this way. Or this way.
Or that."

He stamped his foot and burst into tears.

" I don't want to be told I can do it this way or that.
I want to be told the *right* way. *The* way."

At a later stage of development, I remember the under-
graduates of a woman's college being furious when Sturge
Moore informed them that there were no general principles
in art. They were studying English literature, and his
pronouncement upset all their notebooks.

Later still, though with even clearer motives, one year a
deputation of teachers at the Oxford Festival of Spoken
Verse, perturbed by the fact that different judges seemed to
like different things, came to ask us as a body what we
wanted. What we wanted! as if ten poets could ever be
unanimous about the detail of their art. It is difference
and variety that keep art alive. The teachers wanted to
systematize it, to get it stereotyped, so that they could teach
what paid.

Yet the ten judges were always agreed on the best work. We fought over the detail of lesser performances, but the winners always chose themselves.

You can no more expect unanimity in art than in life. Agreement on broad principles, yes. (Sturge Moore was trying to get those spoon-fed girls to realize that an individual work of art exists in its own terms, that it makes its own world and its own laws and must be judged by them. They resented this, because they were docile, because they still wanted to know *the* view, the right view : what he said would force them to rely on their own judgment, and make their work much harder. But certain broad principles are common to all the arts.)

Let us consider briefly the broad principles which govern the art of speaking verse.

These principles will at first be accepted only among those who understand the art. You will hear a great deal of nonsense from the general public about this as about every form of art. This is not because the public cannot recognize first-class art. It does—often : and the sad fact is, the simpler and less educated the audience, the surer its response. This is only to be expected, in view of the sort of education most of us get. The taste of children and other people uncorrupted by bad education, while it may not readily distinguish good from bad, will always respond to what is good, provided that its subject-matter does not lie beyond the range of their understanding : sometimes even when it does.

I could give a score of examples of this truth, but I must not let myself be diverted from the point, which is that very many people, having been educated away from their natural taste for rhythm and the music of words, talk nonsense about verse speaking and want it to be something which destroys its very essence.

Letters of complaint are forever coming in to the B.B.C. that verse is spoken on the air " mournfully " or " in a special sort of voice," backed by demands that it shall be spoken in a " manly " way, so that listeners can understand at once what it is all about.

When one analyses these complaints, and questions the complainants further, one finds that they want the verses talked and chatted : read with all the emphasis on the sense, and none on the rhythm : read, in fact, as if they were prose. Of course this is what they want ! In school, they have been taught to paraphrase poetry, to " get the sense " of it, to "put it into their own words". They have been regaled with notes on the references in it, and what this or that word or expression means. Small wonder they have lost touch with the music of words. Small wonder they ask that verse should be made to sound as much like prose as possible.

But this way of speaking verse robs it of its essential character. It might as well be prose. I have yet to meet the poet who would not prefer a rhythmic, even a sing-song reading of his work to one which heavily underlined the various aspects of its subject-matter and broke it up into unrelated pieces. In a good poem, the rhythm *is* the sense. The telling word is in the telling place in the line. The beat falls where it is needed. Rhythm and sense are one.

The reasons why an ordinary conversational method will not do for speaking verse were perfectly set forth by the late John Drinkwater in gramophone records made for the Columbia Company close on twenty years ago.

The gist of what he said was this. In ordinary conversation, the actual words are not as important as the tone in which they are spoken. To grunt in heavy and funereal tones, " It's a nice day, isn't it ? " will convey less than cheerful but inarticulate cries. But in poetry every word is important. Every word, in its position, is chosen deliberately by the poet : therefore every word must be sounded with reference to its position in the line, and to the music of the line.

A conversational inflection, with its jerky up-and-down, bent only on the sense, cannot achieve this. It will introduce stresses and variations which are irrelevant to the total meaning of the line. Drinkwater illustrated this very forcibly by speaking a couple of lines in his beautiful rhythmic voice, and then saying them with a conversational inflection, which lost all their music, ruined their meaning, and made them commonplace.

Ruined their meaning : yes, because the sense is only a part of the meaning. The meaning of a poem is built up of sense and music. Our schools, damn them, have taught as if the meaning were the sense alone. With their paraphrases and their notes and their so-called explanations, they have fostered the notion that a poem means no more than the sense of what it seems to be about.

The truth is that a poem is an indivisible whole made up of words, music, and associations, plus the unique meaning which these things produce when arranged according to a certain plan and in a certain order. Each human soul is unique. Each poem is the record of a unique experience. It voices a meaning which apart from it must remain unsaid.

Hence any way of speaking a poem which neglects the music is bound to miss the meaning : just as to drone the words with no regard for the sense must also miss the meaning. But, of the two, the latter is the lesser fault : since it does recognize and attempt the poem's music. It fails, because the sense and the music are (in good verse) always one.

So the chatty, prosy, matter-of-fact speaking of verse demanded by so many listeners is not verse speaking at all. They demand it because, thanks to the teaching they have received, they know no better. But, in some cases, I must admit, they have been provoked. They are not wholly in the wrong. There is a kind of melancholy and sentimental mooing which sometimes masquerades as verse speaking.

It has been called "the poetry voice." The "poetry voice" is bad, for the simple reason that it is a bad voice. Nobody can speak verse without sustained tone : but the tone need not suggest the howling of a dog or the mooing of a cow in labour. It need not always be in a minor key. Drinkwater's tone was as manly as the most robust rugby three-quarter could desire. The "poetry voice" is unnatural. It argues a sentimental attitude to poetry. It removes it from the sphere of art, where it belongs, to the arty-crafty sphere where nothing belongs. It is heard from middle-aged ladies upon whom life has made insufficient demands, and mistaught schoolgirls whose emotions are not yet in focus. In both classes it is temporarily excusable, but in no one else : and it is always inexcusable in public.

I speak feelingly on this point, for a defect of my own speaking is a tendency to fall into a minor key. I hope I have never been guilty of the "poetry voice" : but I certainly do not use a conversational voice. I use a different tone from the tone in which I speak prose : a sustained tone : a tone that enables me to phrase the line as the poet has written it.

Poetry is heightened speech. We must not read it as if we were reading Bradshaw, or even an exciting paragraph from the newspaper. Anyone who has heard a really good speaker of verse—Robert Speaight, for instance, John Laurie, or Felix Aylmer among the actors ; Celia Johnson ; Christopher Hassall or Cecil Day Lewis, among the poets ; V. Clinton-Baddeley, whom W. B. Yeats taught to broadcast his poems—anyone who has heard speaking of this quality never again demands the chit-chat method. John Gielgud is not asked to speak Shakespeare's verse as if it were prose. The audience at the Old Vic did not jib at the organ tones of the late Ion Swinley. The eloquence of these fine players, even in the theatre, where an audience must get the sense of what is happening, is miles removed from the chit-chat analysis of sense alone. Why do none of our friends complain ? Perhaps costume and character are held to excuse their speaking !

A certain degree of formality, then, is necessary to the speaking of verse. The voice must be capable of sounding, in their purest form, the vowels which colour the line, and clearly articulating the consonants which give it movement. It must be capable of many shades of emphasis, more subtle than those of ordinary conversation, since it is not permitted conversational inflections. It must be able to sustain the tone throughout a phrase, as a singer sustains his tone, but less obtrusively, and without dwelling on vowels and syllables as a singer must in obedience to the musical score. In a word, it must be highly controlled, so that it may carry out the mind's instructions.

And, before the voice begins, these instructions must be there. The speaker must have felt and thought every line before the voice can get to work. Mind and voice must be at the poem's service. The job is to pass on the meaning of the poem : not only the sense, not only the music, but the meaning made by the marriage of both. The right approach is not, as sometimes and very vulgarly, " What can I do with this ? " but " What does this say ? " What did the poet mean ? When I know, how can I pass it on, so that others shall know ?

And now, at last, comes the answer to the second of the two questions raised in the last chapter, whether it is sacrilege to use poetry in order to develop the speaking voice. We don't do anything of the kind. We speak a poem for the poem's sake, learning to speak by speaking. The only way of learning to do a thing is to do it.

The work we put in at this many-sided task of speaking verse will give us humility, and improve all our faculties. At the end of it, we shall be better speakers of verse, and, incidentally, better speakers of everything else. You can't learn to do a thing well with your voice without your voice's reaping the benefit.

Caruso once said that nothing so soon repaid attention and showed such quick results as the human voice. He had reason to know. The practice of speaking verse does more for the ear, and so for the voice, and so again for the ear and the voice, than any other form of speech. It is a noble end in itself, and, like most noble ends, it confers other benefits by the way.

CHAPTER VIII

Meaning

FITZ : Horror on horror's head !
LANDLORD : Wotjemean ?
G. B. Shaw : *Passion, Poison, and Petrifaction.*

LET us leave the question of speech as performance, and return to its immediate purpose of communicating meaning in everyday life.

If I seem to insist from time to time on an idealistic view, it is because we can never come to harm by looking for first principles. On the contrary, we will go astray unless we do. The ultimate purpose of speech is not that you and I should be able to ask each other to pass the salt, but that one human soul should be able to make itself known to another.

Life is a lonely business. We dare not miss any chance of communicating with our fellow-travellers, or neglect any means of understanding and being understood, of sharing with them what we feel and know.

There are two great means of sharing experience : art and speech : the records man makes of what he sees and feels, and the words he can exchange with his contemporaries. The works of art are timeless. They speak from one generation to another. Whatever their form, painting, sculpture, music, poetry, drama, architecture, pottery, they speak of what is unchanging in life. But we are not limited to this kind of communication. We have an immediate, you-to-me medium, the medium of speech. How do we use it ?

For the most part, very badly. The cynic who said that speech was given us in order that we might conceal our thoughts was taking advantage of this fact. If we did not use the gift badly, there would be no point in his remark.

As I suggested in an earlier chapter, our inadequacy in revealing ourselves and expressing what we have to say has two main branches. We make insufficient use of the resources of the language, and we misuse our voices. For a few minutes, let us look at the first failing.

The late Stephen Leacock, in a book published after his death, named *How To Write*, began by saying that we can write if we can think, but that most people cannot think. He did not mean by this that they could not feel : but to have feelings and prejudices, to have things going on in one's mind, is not the same thing as being able to think. To think means to see objects and the relationships between them so clearly that we can find the right words for both, and express the whole process so that anyone else can recognize exactly what we are talking about. Recognize exactly—not get a vague idea which he has to supplement by an effort of his own sympathetic understanding. The exact language of the sciences and of philosophy is the statement of clear thought. When the language is not clear, the thought has not been clear.

It is safe to say that when a thing will not readily go into words, it is because we have not really thought it out. When I was broadcasting to schools, I found it possible to go into quite complex questions about writing in its various forms, provided I had thought them out clearly enough to put them in simple words. When I could not do this, when I found difficulty in getting the thought down on paper, it was because it was not in the true sense a thought at all, but only a feeling, something relatively vague, unfocused, unreasoned.

I know, of course, that some of the things in our minds are very difficult to pin down in words, but they are not *thoughts* until we have so expressed them. This is as true of the poet as of the philosopher or the logician. The exact image that symbolizes the flying vision, the exact definition that clarifies the idea : both are thought, in the sense

Stephen Leacock intended, and to be able to think them is to be able to write them. And, of course, to be able to say them.

For if the thing can be said, it can be written : and if it can be written, it can be said. Speech is commonly much less exact than writing, because we have the help of gesture, tone of voice, facial expression, and our listener's sympathy. But we allow it to be far too inexact : and when we have to speak to more than one person, when we are conveying a message or an argument, when we are speaking publicly, we dare not be inexact.

By exactness I do not mean any form of pedantry. I mean simply the capacity to give another person the impression we wish, no more and no less. If we wish them to do a thing, the capacity to inform them just what it is, If we wish to give them a piece of information, the capacity to give them precisely that piece of information. If we wish to present an argument, the capacity to present each stage in it so that it will be understood and followed.

A platitude ? Easy ? Don't you believe it. The human aptitude to misunderstand is infinite.

" I told 'er, so clear as clear, but she took it up wrong."

" I'm after explainin' it till I'm black in the face, but sure. they don't understand."

And in each case the speaker is aggrieved, and feels that he has done all that is possible. But there are two parties to every misunderstanding : and, since the aim of speech is to communicate, the means of communication must be suited to the recipient. It is no good speaking to people in language which they do not understand. And through paucity of vocabulary, through failure to move from one level of expression to another, this is what we very often do.

I was once organizing a village fête in Devon. One of the items, a novelty in the district, was a baby show. For some time the entries were slow to come. One mother refused to enter her very fine and healthy baby, because his great-aunt had said that, if he were passed over, 'twould be a stigma. The mother didn't know what a stigma was, but she wasn't taking any chances.

Then a second mother came to us one morning in apparent indignation.

" I was minded to put my baby in for your show," she exclaimed, " but I ain't going to now."

" Oh, Mrs. Smale, I'm sorry to hear that. Why not ? "

" Well, I've heard tell you strips the poor little toads stark naked and lays 'em out 'pon the grass."

We searched anxiously for the origin of this disquieting rumour, and at last tracked it down. The Vicar in his sermon on the preceding Sunday had alluded to the ancient Greek custom of exposing delicate infants on the hillside !

In each case, disparity of vocabulary had caused a misunderstanding. One lady thought a stigma was some sort of disease (at least, I suppose that is what she must have thought) because the word was new to her. The other, or her informant, probably got as much from this one of the learned vicar's sermons as from any other, because he had not the sense to choose a form of communication suited to his hearer's understanding. I daresay she didn't listen to the rest, but this striking passage about babies caught her attention momentarily, and she related it to the forthcoming show.

It would be easy to pile up examples of verbal misunderstanding, some trivial and amusing, such as these, others of tragic importance. One might glance at the theological difficulties occasioned by the mistranslation of Greek or archaic words : the confusion resulting from the fact that the Greek *polemios*, meaning " enemy of the state," and *echthros*, " person hateful to one, personal enemy," were both rendered by the same English word " enemy " : the happy muddle chronicled by R. H. Mottram in his *Spanish Farm* trilogy, where the phrase " *une vierge esquintée* " was understood to mean a maiden seduced, instead of, as was the case, a statue of the Blessed Virgin knocked crooked : the different interpretations put upon the same word by different people, when its exact meaning was left doubtful by the context : and numberless other instances.

I once attended a series of meetings of psychologists and psychiatrists, my function being to discover and proclaim the occasions when they were using the same words with different meanings.   My interventions were frequent. From the first, we found that the chief terms were being understood differently by each member, according to his school of thought.   Such terms as " consciousness," " the unconscious," " reality," " subjective," which were cardinal to the whole discussion, meant different things to everyone present.   It took me till the fifth meeting to pin down what one member meant by subjective and objective reality in terms which the rest could get hold of—and to do that I had to make drawings on a blackboard.   And these were professionals, accustomed to say what they meant in exact and scientific terms.

Such terms, in point of fact, are often the worst of all. The use of a long word often absolves us from having to think clearly.   Unless very sharply defined and limited, technical terms are the prime question-beggars.   Jargon of all kinds, loose, ill-fitting, long words whose resonance hides their emptiness, are the refuge of the incompetent and the lazy everywhere.   The absurd bits of Civil Service English on pp. 9-10, each designed to conceal the fact that it said nothing, are good examples of this sort of thing.

Jargon is not always used in order to mystify.   A Civil Servant became so much the slave of it that he wrote : " The latest developments in the war situation have tended to divide the Mediterranean into watertight compartments."   It fell to my lot occasionally to sort out and put into English the reports drawn up within this or that Ministry : and what I can't tell you about trends and tendencies and the swing of the pendulum isn't knowledge.

Trends and tendencies are not, of course, Civil Service copyright. Books about English literature love them dearly. They come a close second to influences and periods, and mean as little.

This is not to say that the words in themselves have no meaning. They have, and, when each is in its right place, no other words will do. But they are too often used loosely and lazily in order to make convenient and thought-less generalizations which save us from taking the trouble to find out the truth. They are rubber stamps, like the stock phrases used in newspapers by men who have to write at top speed and who know their readers will never bring them to book.

"Due to the prevailing inadequacy of the means of transport, it has been found impracticable to effect the desired transfers of sections of the population between the scheduled areas."

In other words, there weren't enough trains, so they couldn't move the people they wanted to move.

"The case may be classified as a progressive compulsive retrogression to pre-pubescent fantasy states, conditioned by recurrent anxiety neurosis, with marked dissociations."

May it? This clot of jargon means—as far as there can be any meaning in a sentence which talks about progressive retrogression—that recurring attacks of anxiety divide the patient's mind in two, and so he tends to console himself more and more with nursery make-believe.

To have the use of an exact vocabulary, however small, is a great asset. In the world of to-day it is of the first importance that we should be able to make our own meaning clear and understand the thoughts of others.

"Why can't you say what you *mean* !"

In that age-old cry, which we first heard in the nursery, echoes and re-echoes the need of humanity to be told clearly, to understand. Sometimes the person addressed can't say what he means because he doesn't really know, he hasn't thought. Sometimes he knows, but doesn't want to say. Sometimes he can't say, because his command of words is poor : and misunderstanding and unhappiness follow.

Augustine Birrell said once that one of the best mottoes for life was " Love me and tell me so." Bless his heart— there is a great deal of truth in this. Life is too short to waste in unspoken emotions, and there is no human being that does not need a boost at some time or other. But the implication spreads even wider. To love, we have to think. To tell, we have to be able to tell.

" Why can't you say what you *mean* ! "

Why indeed ?

As always, we are brought back to the problems of personality. The impulses to speech rise in the mind, and their character and quality depend on how the mind reacts to its experience. But even this basic aspect of speech is not beyond our help. The personality can be helped to adjust itself to the world, so that what it wishes to say is honest and open-hearted. It can be helped, too, to translate its impulses into speech that will express them clearly : and it can be helped to overcome any defects in the instrument of speech, the voice, whose character in turn depends upon the personality.

In studying the problems of speech, we cannot go too deep.

CHAPTER IX

Voice

Deeper and deeper still.   Aria from *Jephthah.*

WHEN we come to consider the instrument of speech, we have to go as deep as sympathy and insight can take us.

I met a lady once, sensitive, able, strikingly intelligent, a successful organizer, yet apparently without trace of bossiness or interference.   She seemed at all points well adjusted to her world.   One thing puzzled me, her voice.   It should have been a contralto, or a warm mezzo.   Instead, it was strained, hard, and as much as three semitones above its proper pitch.

I wondered at first if the fault lay with the successful organizer, but, as I say, the lady was not at all of the hard and bossy type.   I wondered if all the activity might not be an escape from inner tension.   At last our talk came round to the subject of voices, and I asked if she knew her voice was too high.

The answer came at once.

" When I was at school, I was terribly anxious to sing the chief part in an operetta, instead of another girl.   It lay too high for me, but I got it.   That's how I strained my voice : and it's stayed too high ever since."

It seemed a good explanation : yet it wasn't.   Before anything could be done to help, a far deeper question had to be dragged out and inspected.   Why was she so anxious to sing the part, instead of the other girl ?   And, deeper still, of what inner attitude was that competitive anxiety the symptom ?

Once these questions were faced—and it took quite a time to disinter the answers—the lady's voice dropped a whole tone.   Even so, it still needed trained attention.

A student at a stage school was bothered by a tightness and hardness in what was naturally a beautiful voice. The following conversation took place :—

" At school, I worked terribly hard at speech, and was always in the final. Twice I missed the first prize by only half a mark. I was terribly disappointed."

" Yes, it was bad luck. But why did you mind so much?"

" I felt ashamed."

" What, of being only half a mark behind the winner, out of the whole school ? "

" Yes."

" But why ? "

" I felt it was my fault."

" That she was judged to be just that little bit better than you ? "

" Yes. If I'd worked a bit harder, I might have won."

Now we had the clue. The student was over-anxious, needed the testimony of prizes and results to justify her existence. Further questions showed parents who were possessively proud of her and wanted her to be always first in everything she attempted : whose ambition for her she thought she could not live up to, and so felt guilty and inferior.

The first step was to suggest that judges were not infallible, and, if she came so near the first prize, another judge might have preferred her. Next, far more important, that the question was not whether she or another girl ranked first, but did each speak her poem as well as she possibly could ? The responsibility was to the poem, not to anything or anybody else.

Then, when some degree of relaxation had come from thinking about these points, the fundamental question could be tackled, and something done to ease the tension of anxiety expressed in the tension of the voice. Of course, the help of a trained teacher was available all the time, on the purely technical side.

One or two more cases may be quoted briefly, as a stimulus to this line of thought, in case it is unfamiliar to some readers.

A singer, imprisoned in a severe emotional dilemma, began to suffer increasingly from a constriction in his throat, and for a period of several months had to give up singing. A partial release from the dilemma, plus a more constructive way of looking at it, restored his voice.

A boy developed in his teens a magnificent baritone voice. His parents rigidly opposed any idea of music as a career, because a relation who was a singer drank and came to a bad end. The boy had attack after attack of tonsillitis until his voice disappeared, and, in this drastic and destructive way, he had got rid of his problem.

A man who disliked and feared another man who was more successful, and, so he thought, patronized him, forgot the second man's name every time he had to refer to him or to introduce him to other people, and, forcing himself to remember, developed a stammer and could not get the name out.

This last is like the case of the child who could not say the letter beginning her hated younger sister's name until the consultant invited her to say "*Blast* Betty." Hundreds of instances can be quoted of speech difficulties and voice difficulties which are due to no defect in the organs concerned, but arise from inner causes.

A singer produced a tight and metallic tone on the vowel of a girl's name which occurred in one of his songs. The discovery, and admission by the singer, that the name had painful associations for him, eased the difficulty.

Another singer frequently went sharp on one note in Handel's aria "Where'er you Walk," from *Semele*. Inquiry revealed that when studying the song with his first teacher, he had once missed the note. The teacher had been very sarcastic, and the beginner's subsequent anxiety caused such tension and excess of effort that he sang off the key.

All troubles and difficulties of this kind can be dealt with most easily at the start of life, in school. They lie within the domain of common sense, and any teacher who has once understood the relation of voice to character can detect and remedy them before they become inveterate. But the trained teacher has the advantage, because he or she is accustomed to look out for such things, and has learned the best way to deal with them. It is good to pick up such sympathetic understanding by the light of nature, but even better to acquire it as part of the teacher's equipment. For every one teacher who has it naturally, fifty can be taught it.

And when we come to physical defects and difficulties, the trained teacher is essential. Having myself been confronted in class with stammerers and sufferers from cleft palate, I know well the problems which they set, and the helplessness of the average teacher to offer more than kindness and patience. I had, too, the pain of seeing one stammerer made very much worse by the practice of an elderly master who, asking questions round the form, gave him even less time to answer than the others, remorselessly saying " Next," in the belief that " the boy could get it out well enough if he had to."

This sort of thing is less likely to happen nowadays, and the advice of the speech therapist is sought as a matter of course. But too often the therapist is the only qualified teacher of speech, and is given none but cases of organic or very severe functional difficulty. Good speech, clear speech, musical speech, voice as an index of personality, are not considered at all. Even when admitted to be desirable, they are supposed to happen by the light of nature, or as Acts of God. That they can and should be fostered, encouraged, and developed : that many a harsh voice is a beautiful voice misused : that even the least pleasing voice may be improved, often with a minimum of help, provided the helper is skilled : that good and musical speech is an essential part of English teaching : this does not enter the average English teacher's head at all.

Anyone who has taught English knows from experience the extraordinary fillip given to the work by the production of a school play. Acting is at last recognized as a part of education. When I first taught, the older masters used to crab and hinder the play in every way they could. Their objections were that it interfered with work, and that it gave boys swelled head.

Helping, very unskilfully, in play production, taught me a lot. I learned the right approach to boys I had failed with before. I found the English work of the cast improved by about thirty per cent. I saw many a boy who had hitherto been a nonentity blossom into social success and self-confidence through the discovery—his own and the school's—that he could act. I learned too the joy of working hard on a job with happy and willing collaborators.

Had I known anything about production : had I known how to help the boys use their voices : had I undergone what should be part of the basic equipment of every teacher of English : then we might really have got somewhere. (I had a colleague who was quite brilliant in grouping and movement, but left the dialogue to me.) As it was, I had to muddle along by the light of Nature.

Too much English teaching muddles along by the light of Nature. We know enough now to be able to train teachers of English to help, positively and creatively, the development of their pupils. Schools of speech and drama are every year turning out scores of competent young men and women who can produce plays, teach good speaking, and who know enough about speech therapy to hand on to the therapist those cases which are beyond the reach of the training (not inconsiderable) which they themselves have received.

This knowledge should not be confined to specialist teachers of speech and drama. *It should be part of the equip-*

ment of every specialist teacher of English. Or, if you prefer to put it the other way on, every teacher of speech and drama should also be a teacher of English, and vice versa. (That would meet the wishes of the Norwood Committee ?)

Alternatively, every school of a hundred and more pupils should have a specialist teacher of speech and drama on the staff : and every school should have the services of one as a visiting member of the staff.

I do not care how it is put : but, for motives of economy, and because English is one and indivisible, I prefer my own comprehensive description that every specialist teacher of English should be able to produce plays and show his pupils how to speak. The bare minimum is that, even if he can't teach the use of the voice, he should be able to use his own.

The objections most frequently raised by opponents of speech teaching are (*a*) that speaking is " natural," that we can all speak, and the less conscious we are of the process the better ; (*b*) that trained speech is " artificial " and " unnatural " and " affected."

Of course speaking is natural. So is walking—but it has to be learned, and very laboriously learned. It is an art. No one is born able to walk. Almost all of us can walk, but some people walk very badly. They walk badly for organic reasons, because they are lame or knock-kneed or bandy. Or they walk badly because they don't take the trouble to walk well, or are neurotic or unhappy, or from some other inner cause. Treatment, orthopaedic, neurological, psychological, can help them to walk. How ? Affectedly ? Artificially ? Unnaturally ? No : *naturally*.

It is the same with the voice. Speaking is an art and has to be learned. No one is born able to speak. All training in the use of voice aims at enabling the pupil to use it naturally, freely, without hindrance, for whatever purpose he or she has in mind : and, fundamentally, to reveal the human being who speaks through the voice.

Not until they try to say something on a stage or platform, or to speak through a microphone, is it realized by the untrained ear how poorly very many people speak. For poorly, read unnaturally : against obstacles, mental and material : ineffectively : lacking power to make their voices carry without strain, and consequent distortion : the defects that perhaps pass unnoticed in conversation magnified cruelly by the effort to speak on a bigger scale, and by the concentration of the listener's attention on the speaker's voice.

A good voice is a natural voice, produced in accordance with Nature's laws. We have come a long way from Nature, some of us, as a result of what we call civilization, and we speak even worse than we walk.

We need a training that will re-educate us and set free our natural powers. Just as the orthopaedist re-educates the cramped and twisted limb, and enables it once more to work naturally, the teacher of speech re-educates the voice which has been misused and enables it to regain its natural music.

It can be done. It is being done, every day, here and there. It ought to be done each day everywhere.

CHAPTER X

Pronunciation

"Don't s'y kike : s'y *kike*." Old Story, *passim*.

THE pronunciation of English varies so widely according to district that rules can be given only for formal speaking. When people act a play or speak at a competitive festival, they can be required to conform to certain standards. In ordinary conversation, we may perhaps be indicted privately for slovenliness, for affectation, "refined" or mincing accents, and so forth : but, as long as we are prepared to face the possible consequences, as set out in earlier chapters, the way we talk is our own affair.

But on stage or platform a stricter rule obtains. The performer is expected to speak Standard English, and Mayfair finds no more favour than Muddlecombe ; probably less. For Muddlecombe, whatever else may be said of it, affects no superiority and is not slovenly in its speech. It is not more acceptable to say "of coo-urse," as does Muddlecombe, than "'v cawce" as does Mayfair (though it is a good deal nearer to the English of Shakespeare) : but Muddlecombe will make the better learner, because its speech mechanism is not shirking anything. In fact, it is working overtime.

The Mayfair tendency is to have as few vowel sounds as possible, and make them all sound approximately alike. The prevailing tone of the voice being a drawl, the vowels are dragged towards it. This form of speech is not content with making no distinction between *floor* and *flaw* : it drags the -ure in words like *sure*, *pure*, etc., into *yaw* (shaw, pyaw). It tells you that the idear of geoing for a streoll on the maws is maw th'n it c'n bah. Its -i sounds are pulled out into aaa-ee, with the -ee doing its best to disappear : and it leaves out any consonant which it can't be bothered to articulate, pausing every now and then to intrude an -r where no -r belongs (idear of, Indiar Office). It can't quite manage " cah " for *cow*, but it does almost say " bahndary " for *boundary* : and so on.

Perhaps it is more than a coincidence that this type of speaking is so often allied to complacency and unadventurousness of mind. It is certainly an ideal dialect for such temperaments, especially when spoken throatily or with the shallow metallic clatter which competes so successfully with traffic or teacups. As I said, its users are perfectly well entitled to it at home and in the teashop : but it will not do for more public occasions, because, instead of illustrating and taking advantage of the variety of the English language in order to express meaning, as a method of speech it is all the time avoiding its responsibilities.

Of the vices of this way of speaking, the one which is spreading most widely is an inability or an unwillingness to distinguish between -aw and -or. The distinction is clear, though it need not be strongly emphasized. We need not say " morrre " with certain Scots, or " mower " with some of the Western counties, or " moore " with others : but we must not say " maw." We need not *sound* the -r, as Mr. Joseph Macleod is at pains to do : but our pronunciation should show that it is there.

Here is an exercise for making this distinction, used in teaching students at one of the principal schools of speech and drama :—

> *A daw with sore claws on a door*
> *Saw some crumbs in a flaw on the floor.*
> *He got more in his maw*
> *On the floor, from the flaw,*
> *Than when perched with sore claws as before.*

To say " with saw claws on a daw " is as silly as " with sore clors on a door." Anyone who can naturally and easily distinguish between the sounds in that is not going to have any trouble with this problem.

Mayfair's intruded -r (idear of), which twenty years ago would have been condemned as a gross vulgarism, has also spread to other places, including, on occasion, the announcers' room at the B.B.C. There is no mystery about it. Children, learning to speak, find it easier to insert the r than to keep a gap between two vowels. It is quite easy to say " idea of," but even easier to say " idear of."

Some officials of the B.B.C. have defended the practice by comparing it to the use of the *liaison* in French. But the Frenchman observes a rigid and definite rule for his *liaisons*. He doesn't just pop one in here and there to save trouble. He doesn't run on a consonant to an aspirated vowel. (We used to madden the French teacher at my preparatory school by saying "lezzzharicots." He shows himself capable of making a gap between two vowels whenever he wishes Yet the announcer who can correctly pronounce " naive " will say " idear of," a form for which there is no grammatical justification whatever.

I agree wholeheartedly that the value of grammar can very easily be overrated. Grammar, as the late Stephan Leacock admirably put it, is only a post-mortem on usage. No mere code of rules can or should restrain the natural growth of language as given to it by the people who use it. If the English-speaking race decides to say " idear of," then " idear of " will become good usage and will have to be taught. But that day has not yet come, and, for the present, teachers of speaking do all they can to stamp it out from every form of speech as performance.

Some sounds are hard to make. Everyone has his or her own pet difficulties. Let me confess to having trouble with the words *library* and *literary* when I am on the platform. R's as a rule don't bother me, but I cannot say " Lalalalalalala " nearly fast enough. The quick passage in *Largo al Factotum*, from " The Barber of Seville," is quite beyond me :—

Ah, bravo Figaro, bravo bravissimo,
Ah, bravo Figaro, bravo bravissimo ;

on the other hand, I can continue it,

Fortunatissimo, fortunatissimo,
Fortunatissimo della citto,

very much faster. This means that my control is only partial.

Why does one need control ? In order to speak in public. What if one doesn't want to speak in public ? Then in order to speak clearly, and be understood by all kinds of people : quite apart from the pleasure which comes from the use of that most rewarding of human faculties, the voice.

The pinched, refined " o " of Mayfair is the natural symbol of a closed mind and an ungenerous attitude to life. It would of course be absurd to suggest that all who pinch their o's suffer from these defects. Nine out of ten have caught the disease by imitation : but the mannerism is that of a privileged order holding on tight to its privileges. It is the speech of tension, afraid to relax and let go. It is also the speech of laziness, unwilling to use its lips and make the necessary round O. And, unfortunately, it has come to be the mark of a social class, copied by those who wish to be thought members of that class, and so is not easy for the teacher to cure.

The short *a* of the North (*a* in *castle* sounded like *a* in *hat*) has the drawback, in formal speech, of impoverishing the music of verse or period by limiting the vowel sounds, and not giving the breadth of tone intended by the writer. Should we say " soft " or " sawft " ? " Often " with the *t*, or " off'n," or " awf'n " ? Here personal taste has more play, but for formal purposes the first will usually be preferred in each case.

In general, the tendency in formal speech will be towards everything that makes for variety and gives actor or verse-speaker the fullest opportunities for colour and resonance.

Here are a very few examples, chosen to give practice in sounds that are either difficult or apt to be distorted. Mayfair, as we have seen, is rude to the second syllable of its own name, and tries to call it -fah.

> *It isn't fair, said the polar bear,*
> *For people to stand and stare.*
> *It isn't fair and I've had my share,*
> *Go look at the beasts over there.*

Mayfair would call a tower a tah :—

> *Above the lowly plants it towers,*
> *The fennel with its yellow flowers,*
> *And in an earlier age than ours*
> *Was gifted with the wondrous powers*
> > *Lost vision to restore.*
> > (*Longfellow*).

Mayfair tries to call a fire a fah, and in another twenty years will probably succeed :—

> *There are several things I admire,*
> *A church with a fine tall spire,*
> *Ladies in handsome attire,*
> *Pretty dumb cows in a byre,*
> *Greyhounds with sinews like wire,*
> *A hearth with a nice bright fire.*
> *These are the things I admire.*

If you have any trouble with clear articulation, try these, slowly at first so as to get them clear and accurate, then faster, and finally, as fast as you can go :—

> *Kitty my love, will you marry me ?*
> *Kitty my love, will you go ?*
> *Kitty my love, will you marry me ?*
> *Either say yes or say no.*

You will find that you have to slow up a bit on the last line, if people are to hear what you are saying.

Now this :—

Betty Botter bought some butter, " But," she said. " this butter's
    bitter :
If I put it in my batter, it will make my batter bitter.
But a bit of better butter, better than the bitter butter,
Will make my batter better." So she bought a bit of butter,
Better than the bitter butter, and made her bitter batter better.
So 'twas better Betty Botter bought a bit of better butter.

Similarly, to repeat as fast as you can " Many men making much money " will do you good besides amusing you.

These, and scores of exercises like them, are more than tongue-twisters. Their use is to increase the mobility and alertness of one's speaking, to give one control over the mechanism by which it comes. The athlete who develops his muscles and his powers of co-ordination may at first think it strange to apply similar methods to the improvement of the means whereby he manifests his personality to the world, but he will not be surprised, once he has admitted the idea, that exercise should develop this faculty too. A fit mind in a fit body demands that the bodily expression of the mind should be fit—fit to express fully and clearly what the mind is thinking.

This short book is not a treatise on how to speak. For that I have no qualification. It is instead a plea for the necessity of good and clear speaking, and an insistence that it can be achieved as soon as the country decides that it wants it and turns to those from whom it can be had.

CHAPTER XI

What We Need.

*Every human soul is unique, for none other can
satisfy the same need in God.*   W. B. Yeats.

THE English teaching we need is one that will give
energy and inspiration to every kind of life, spiritual,
mental, and physical.   It is a creative teaching.   It will not
only awaken the creative ability in the child, but will make
him grow in stature as a human being.   It will be a teaching
which the artist can endorse, the writer, the philosopher,
the priest.   It will be alive.

Nothing but the highest aim will do.   Nothing but the
most difficult endeavour is possible.   And, by a paradox
which always proves to be true, the most difficult, once
firmly attempted, proves easiest in the end.

Too often the enemy of the child's progress is the teacher.

" Oh, that's above their heads."

" Don't try to run before you can walk."

" They'll never understand that."

" It's easy to see *you* have no experience of the classroom."

" Children of this age group aren't capable of that."

Ladies and gentlemen, *it is not true*.   I have proved it,
seen it proved, heard it proved, been told by those who
have proved it, again and again and again.   The uncorrupted minds of children (uncorrupted by timid and partial
teaching) can understand almost anything *once their imagination is roused and kindled*.   And children have the most
generous and inflammable imagination in the world.   He
who is himself on fire can always light it.   It is killed by
the pedant, the timid, the unbelieving.   Trust a child's
mind, and you can tell him anything.   Doubt it, and he
will justify your doubt.

I am not a theorist. I have served twelve years in the classroom, I have given close on a hundred broadcasts to schools (a service in which the results are remorselessly checked), I have been speaking on literary subjects to boys and girls, of all ages from ten to nineteen, for fourteen years : and I know what can be got over to them—everything : everything you know yourself, and have proved, and can talk about.

The most searching technical question I was ever asked came from a sixteen-year-old boy at Winchester. The best collective appreciation of a passage from James Joyce's *Finnegans Wake* came from a large class of ten-to-twelve-year-olds at a boys' county school near London. I have had from girls of eleven questions so penetrating in their honesty and simplicity that there have been tears at the back of my eyes as I tried in all humility to reply. I have had letters from schoolboy and schoolgirl listeners which asked for all the honesty and all the insight I could command— and more. Time and again, in talking to boys and girls, my own imagination has caught fire from their flame.

Am I an idealist ? An optimist ? Yes, passionately, always. In teaching I do not admit of failure. We may not succeed in doing what we want or expect, but if we will trust and go ahead, making use of every atom of skill and experience we have, and remembering always the idiom and the interests of those we are trying to teach, we will achieve something. Something good, something creative, something in the child's own terms. Some impulse to create, some spark of wondering appreciation, some discovery, however gradual, astonished, and delayed, that there are active pleasures for him in the use and enjoyment of his own language.

Nor are these perceptions confined to children. I could show you letters from farm labourers, from the wives of working men, from all manner of people who have had no fit opportunity to discover what their own tongue holds for them, but who show in their own discovery of it a humility, an enthusiasm, and a pure taste which would abash many a graduate teacher of English.

If I point out that these contacts are almost all made through the medium of the speaking voice, I run the risk of appearing to pay myself a compliment. That cannot be helped. No one is more conscious than I of my vocal shortcomings : but it is legitimate to point out that if my voice were physically hampered by stammer or malformation, were so constricted by self-consciousness or nervous tension that it could express neither my belief in what I said nor my feelings of friendship and co-operation with my listeners, the contact would not have been made, or would have been reduced in effect. What can happen as a result of something in a voice only those who have experience of such things can tell. The voice is the most subtle conveyor of what is in the speaker, for it speaks to more than the hearer's conscious mind. I could give you instance after instance of this. So could many a singer whom I might name. The importance of voice can hardly be exaggerated ; the value of an expressive voice, the handicap of one that is harsh or unsympathetic.

And, except in cases of physical disease, no voice need remain harsh and unsympathetic. Any and every voice that is not pathologically abnormal can be taught to sound in harmony with its owner's spirit.

But suppose the spirit is harsh and unpleasant ? Suppose the harsh voice truly represents it ? To answer that we must ask what went wrong at that man's or woman's school, that no one took the case in hand, got through to the spirit, and cured its trouble ?

Mr. Chuter Ede, at the time of writing, the able, robust and genial Parliamentary Secretary to the Ministry of Education, tells a pleasant story of his early days as a teacher.

A pompous official visitor, coming into his class of seventy small boys, observed patronizingly, " You are teaching a very large class here, Mr. Ede."

" No, sir," replied the young teacher. " I'm not teaching them anything. I earn the thirty-five shillings a week you give me by stopping them from smashing the furniture."

Every practising teacher knows that the first real reform (in 1945) is not to raise the school leaving age, but to reduce the number of children in each class. This less spectacular aim has not commended itself to Parliament, but Parliament is not made up of teachers, and has never shown itself benevolently interested in their problems.

Of course a child's personal problems remain unsolved, perhaps undetected, in classes of more than thirty. Of course there is no time to straighten out difficulties of speech and voice, unless these reach the degree of positive abnormality, sufficient to hinder the child's progress in class. One might go further and say that the effort required to keep such classes going at all is enough to dry up the creative powers of the teacher and harden his voice to an admonitory parade-ground bark.

But let us stick to observed facts. What we want is something that can be done, for a start, right away, now, with conditions as they are.

Even a large class can be interested by being set to speak suitably chosen verses in chorus. Girl students of eighteen and nineteen have held and delighted mobs of fifty and more unruly small boys by persuading them to say together exciting, bloodthirsty, or amusing verses, particularly if they involved rapid patter and changes of pace and volume. No one who has not seen this done in a teeming city elementary school can believe the speed of the results, the enjoyment of the children, and—often—the excellent quality of the mass readings. Solo lines can be given to promising individuals, gross mispronunciations corrected, real dramatic and musical ability uncovered, a score of promising creative openings made. Untold good can be done : there is no lack of evidence.

But the teacher must know his or her job. It is no work for the amateur. It needs sympathy, imagination, and training. The training is on tap, and can be given. It should be given. Why is it withheld ?

Perhaps, the world being what it is, I ought to say that I have no financial interest in any school or system of training, no personal axe to grind. I have only my knowledge, gained from experience, and reinforced every day, of the miracles which good voice teaching can do. I know, in my own life, the joy of learning a little about my voice and how to use it. I look around, I see on all sides the growing power and importance of the spoken word. I see, very often, the difference made to individual lives by the new-found ability to say what they mean, in more ways than one. I savour the pleasures of listening, the adventure of reaching through the voice to the personality behind it. And, jealous for the instrument by which we live, our English tongue, I want to see it not only taught but lived, in all its many-sided colour, energy, and beauty.

I want to see an end of the dreary, ungenerous system whereby the way a person speaks limits his chances of getting on in the world. This system, which hitherto has favoured the well-to-do, might work the other way. Aldous Huxley, in his novel *Antic Hay*, envisages a new Shibboleth :—

"The Red Guards will stop people in the street and ask them to say some such word as ' towel.' If they call it ' towel,' like you and your friends, Mr. Gumbril, why then . . . " Mr. Bojanus went through the gestures of pointing a rifle and pulling the trigger ; he clicked his tongue against his teeth to symbolise the report . . . " That'll be the end of them But if they say ' tèaul,' like the rest of us, Mr. Gumbril, it'll be ' Pass Friend and Long Live the Proletariat.' Long live Tèaul."

These are artificial distinctions between man and man. We have enough already. There is a celebrated bathing place near Dublin where men of all classes bathe together naked. I remember my fisherman friend and mentor,

Paddy Kennedy, observing with a touch of bitterness that " when men was as God made them, sure yer couldn't tell who was who " : and, carefully brought up little Protestant gentleman's son that I was, I remember being faintly scandalized to observe that this was indeed the case. I was scandalized, not because I was a snob—Paddy was my dearest friend—but because it seemed to me a reversal of the natural order in a society of which I had been encouraged to regard God as the author.

I suspect that many of those who jib at the idea of people being taught to speak good English have at the back of their minds a similar conception, not so crude, but equally childish and indefensible. " It has never been done "— that great watchword of British policy and progress—is strengthened by the feeling that to take pains about the way one speaks is precious, affected, unnatural, and therefore un-English. It is un-English to speak English properly. Un-English, to try to make full use of our heritage. Such a paradox is well in line with our traditions and our practice.

But can it be defended ? Must our speech remain a drab and colourless monotone ? Must we leave it to the foreigner to speak our language picturesquely ? Why is it good form to pass by its richness of vocabulary and its music ? We are our own worst advertisers : are we always to remain so ? Are a handful of actors and a trained speaker or so enough to maintain the repute of English speech ? Must we leave its defence to a Welshman in Parliament, an Irishman in the courts, a Scot everywhere ? Why do we refuse to speak our own language worthily ?

I honestly believe that it is not too much to say that, if we cannot better present our English way of life to the world, it may perish of isolation and in-breeding. The first way to present it, and the best, is by making a good use of our English tongue. A few do it by nature. The rest must be taught.

All can learn.

CHAPTER XII

" Though I speak with the tongues of men and of angels "

ST. PAUL.

A DIFFICULTY which always arises as soon as we talk about teaching English is the definition of teaching. The difficulty is not to define teaching : plenty of people are ready to have a shot at that : but to be sure that the parties to the conversation have the same definition in mind, and agree about its validity. For the moment, therefore, let me put the verb in inverted commas.

I " taught " at a school where the " teaching " was excellent. The speciality of the school was to win scholarships at Eton, Winchester, and other big public schools. This was done by means of Latin and Greek, which we " taught " to a very high standard of accuracy. Boys from the scholarship form of this preparatory school could have gone into the form next to the top at the public school where I was " taught." Their work consisted for the most part in the accurate reproduction of what they had been " taught," but they also acquired a real facility in composition—albeit on rather stereotyped lines. They were " taught " to introduce certain easily memorized idioms into all their compositions ; and I greatly annoyed the authorities, one year when I was given the classical examining to do, by parodying these in the course of my report. However, let me repeat, the " teaching " was excellent. Not only the scholarship results but the subsequent careers of the winners testified to its soundness.

But when I was set to " teach " English, I knew from the first that a very different method was needed ; so different that the same verb could hardly be used to describe it. The examiners had grown tired of finding out what scholarship candidates could be " taught." They wanted to know what they could do on their own. So they set a kind of examination which could not be prepared for in the accepted way. They asked questions in which the candidates could not be coached. They demanded answers which showed personality, individual quality, rather than trained accomplishment. I could not " teach " the answers to such questions. What I had to do was—if possible—to " teach " the boys to answer them. That, in such a school, meant little short of revolution.

You can see the picture. A crowd of well-drilled and subjugated boys had first of all to be kept in order. Vastly in awe of the authorities, they had to be persuaded to accept the ministrations of a very young man unarmed with the authorities' weapons. Next, docile as they were mentally, they had to accept as " teaching " a treatment that threw them on their own resources. They had to be persuaded that it was legitimate for them to have opinions of their own, that these opinions were not only worth having, but worth listening to, and were, incredible though it must seem, what the examiners wanted. And they had to be persuaded that the things we discussed were interesting enough for them to have opinions about.

The English " teaching " which I had to give was therefore quite unlike all the rest of the " teaching " they received. It was, from their point of view, far less satisfactory (until they became resigned and accustomed to it) because it called for a greater effort on their part, and an effort of a kind for which all their previous " teaching " had unfitted them. Mere industry, mere memory-training, would not do. They had to make something for themselves : and, at first, they must have felt they were being asked to make bricks without straw. What kind of " teaching " was this, to offer hard-worked twelve- and thirteen-year-olds.

Many years later, I had to " teach " English by radio.

I had an audience which I could not see, scattered all over the country in places I did not know, speaking all manner of dialects, varying widely in range and standard, about whom the one safe thing to assume was that they knew nothing at all of what I was attempting to " teach " them. Here my task was not to inform (as did the " teachers " of other subjects at the school where I " taught "), nor to stimulate them to reveal themselves by creating something (as I tried to do at the said school), but to awaken interest and if possible hold it.

A fresh definition was needed.   Even then, I did not hit on it for close on four years, when a thing I was asked to do put me on the track.   I was to give three talks on story-telling to children classed as " non-literary "—which, in elementary schools, is decidedly euphemistic.   The talks were part of a series already begun, so that I inherited the set-up, the formula on which they were given.   This con-sisted of two imaginary children, a boy and a girl, played by child actors, who were supposed to question me, and with whom I was to discuss the business in hand.   This formula was considered more lively and easier to listen to than a solo talk.   I disliked it, because it was a fake.   There were no such children, and the stooges who purported to represent them said what the writer of the script, in this case myself, put into their mouths.   I do not like the least hint of dishonesty in dealing with children, however laud-able the motive.   Least of all do I like it at the microphone, because fake is shown up there in all its nakedness.   Still, I accepted the formula.

Then it was suggested to me that I should make the two imaginary children try to tell stories and do it all wrong : make mistakes which I should put right.   This abominable suggestion I rejected with all the violence of which I am capable.   Think of it.   I, whose task was to capture the confidence and interest of listening children, was invited to drive a wedge between them and myself, to make it appear that children could not do anything right by themselves without some superior grown-up to show them how !

That would not even be " teaching " in inverted commas. It would be something quite unprintable—and I all but said so.

But I am glad it happened, for it " taught " me another thing about " teaching," which is that it is a form of co-operation that can only occur when both parties are on the same side. In these talks, " teaching " meant that the children (as represented by the stooges) and I joined together to make something. The fact that I had previous experience of making such things meant that I could help them to shape their intentions more effectively : help them to get it out.

I shall ask you to remember that phrase : *help them to get it out*.

Even if we go no further, then, there are obviously two distinct kinds of " teaching." One is the imparting of information in such a form that the recipient will be able to recall and reproduce it accurately. The other is giving the pupil the stimulus to do something for himself, and helping him to do it. This is less technical : more personal. It will be found to depend less on what the " teacher " knows than on what he is. Is he such as to inspire others with his own interest in what he " teaches " ? Can he help them to " get it out " ?

The first " teacher " puts things in by methods which ensure that they may easily be taken out again for inspection. Sometimes, when the inspection is over, they will not be needed any more ; they may safely be forgotten.

The second " teacher " is the means whereby his pupils may get out that which is in themselves, in a more active and flourishing form than if he had not been there. He sees not only what they are but what they can be, and helps them to be it and to " get it out."

Sometimes I think that the teacher (I have, you observe,

dropped the inverted commas) is no more than a piece of propitious furniture in a room where magical things happen —things which would not happen so well, however, if he were not there, and, in some cases, would not happen at all. He somehow enables the pupil to see himself as he could be, if all the best in him were realized.

To be able to show the pupil this, the teacher must of course have seen it first himself. What is more, he must have divined the line of approach to the pupil—different with each individual—which will prove to the pupil that both are on the same side, and are working together for the same end.

In his book *Invisible Anatomy*, Dr. E. Graham Howe relates a conversation he had with a nurse who was looking after one of his patients. (He is a psychiatrist.) The nurse was in difficulties : she did not feel she understood the patient.

Dr. Howe replied, " There is something more important than understanding her, because that may not be possible either for the nurse or the doctor. Quite honestly, I don't understand her either. The more important question is, ' Do you like her ? ' If you can't do that, give up the case."

In this country, which tends to pride itself on being un-emotional, we prefer to say that the teacher must love his *job*. Perhaps I will not be outraging our national reticence if I say that he must also like his pupils. (You will perhaps have noticed the quotation at the head of the chapter.)

Let us try to see where we have got to.

English is one and indivisible.

The love of English is one and indivisible.

The teaching of English (that is, the communication of this love to others) is one and indivisible.

So far, so good. The teaching of English has many branches. We can " teach " grammar, rule by rule ; we can make pupils parse and analyse : but we can only inspire them with love of English, only inspire them to create and discover for themselves.

What is more, a vivid, live ungrammatical sentence is better writing, better English, than a correct but dull and lifeless one.

This statement will make a number of " teachers " grit their teeth, either because all they feel qualified to do is to instil correctness, or because they are pedants and set adherence to rule above everything else. But I repeat it, as true both in the schoolroom and out of it.

Shaw's immortal line from *The Admirable Bashville*,

" 'E seen me coming and 'e done a bunk,"

is better English than :

" Perceiving my approach, he withdrew rapidly in the opposite direction."

" 'E tries to uppercut me, see ? I jerks me 'ead left, and as 'is elber come up, I slips in close and jabs 'im in the guts."

Better English, sir and madam, than what it might be corrected to by a scandalized " teacher " :

" He endeavoured to deliver an uppercut, do you understand ? I moved my head to the left, and as his elbow came up, leaving him unprotected, I came to close quarters and fetched him a short-armed blow to the abdomen."

Better English, because more vivid, more alive, more appropriate to the theme.* In my classroom or out of it, I should give the first ten out of ten, and the second about three.

The compliment to my teaching which I most value came from an old pupil, John Lehmann, who told a friend that he would always be grateful to me because I never corrected his phrasing or punctuation, and so did not hinder him from forming his own style.

This does not mean that I never corrected anyone's

---

* I do not suggest, needless to say, that a grammatical sentence cannot be as vivid as an ungrammatical. Corrections need bring no loss of vigour.

phrasing or punctuation. I did, often : but only when it made what they were trying to say less intelligible and less effective. Only when, because of it, expression was not doing justice to intention. If anyone in my class had written " 'E tries to uppercut me," etc., I should certainly not have changed anything, since he would have perfectly realized his intention.

To resume, then :—

Good writing or speaking is alive : that is to say, the expression is in perfect harmony with the intention.

Correctness is valuable only as a means to an end, and the end is clear expression.

The imparting of correctness in itself is not teaching.

Now we go further, and become bolder.

The love of English cannot be taught as one can teach correctness. It can only be communicated or inspired.

This brings us back to our central point. The chief means of communication is the human voice.

How many voices communicate exactly what the speaker wishes to say—let alone inspire ?

To inspire, the teacher must love his work, and be able to express his love, and pass it on to others, through his voice. Let us ensure for him that he can do it.

We have seen that speaking is an art. Like walking, it has to be learned. Only after a long series of experiments do we learn to use our legs and our tongue so that they obey our purposes. Left to Nature, we do not always learn either to walk well or to speak well. A good deal is done to correct bad gait and bad posture, but little to improve bad speech. Can we afford, as a nation or as individuals, to let this state of affairs continue ?

Can teachers any longer afford a state of affairs which so often impairs their usefulness ?

May I, in conclusion, point back to the quotation at the head of this chapter ? For " charity " the modern scholar reads " love." The teacher must love his or her job : and that means loving not only the subject, and the teaching of it, but those whom he or she is trying to teach. Only by this threefold enthusiasm, this threefold care, can the inspired result come. In our concern with ways and means, we must never forget the truth which is at the centre of all teaching and all life.

———————

PRINTING BY TUCKER & OXLEY, LTD.